In the name of God, the beneficent, the merciful

ON THE ISLAMIC HIJAB

by

Murtaza Mutahhari

Translated by

Laleh Bakhtiar

مطهری، مرتضی، ۱۲۹۹ ـ ۱۳۵۸ Mutahhari, Murtaza
(مسئله حجاب انگلیسی)

On the Islamic hijab / by Mutahhari
Mutahhari translated by Laleh Bakhtiari.
Tehran: Islamic Propagation Organization.
International Publishing co. ۱۳۸۰-۲۰۰۲

۱۰۸ ص.

ISBN : 978-964-7126-61-8

فهرستنویسی براساس اطلاعات فیپا.

۱. حجاب. الف. بختیار، لاله Bakhtiar Laleh. مترجم. ب. سازمان تبلیغات اسلامی. شرکت چاپ و نشر بین الملل. ج. عنوان. مسئله حجاب انگلیسی د. عنوان: On the Islamic hijab

۵۰۴۹۵۲ م ۶ م / ۲۳۰/۱۷/ BP   ۲۹۷/۶۳۶

۱۳۸۰

کتابخانه ملی

م ۸۰-۲۵۴۱۲

مسئله حجاب
شهید مطهری (انگلیسی)

INTERNATIONAL
PUBLISHING CO.

On the Islamic Hijab
By: Murtaza Mutahhari
Publisher: International Publishing Co.
Third Published: 1386
Printed and bound by: Sepehr Printing House
In 3000 Copies
ISBN: 978-964-7126-61-8
Price: 9000

PUBLISHER'S NOTE

On the basis of ideology of Islam, covering ("*hijab*") for women is considered one of the basic and important principles. Islam's view regarding women is quite different from what the West thinks about women. Islam considers women as half of the body of the society and holds that women, like men, should live with human standards and values.

Western society looks at woman merely through the windows of sexual passion and regards woman as a little being who just satisfies sexual desires. Before everything else the question of sexual passions is set forth even in marriage. Therefore, such a way of thinking results in nothing other than the woman becoming a propaganda and commercial commodity in all aspects of Western life, ranging from those in the mass media to streets and shops. This is the ultimate degree of woman's slavery and fall in Western societies which has no consequence other than corruption and misery. While Islam with the permissibility and opening vast and extensive fields for social activities for women, has restricted sexual activities and liberties. With exact and all-round laws it has established a reasonable and just balance in the context of woman's individuality and social life.

The first practical issue in this connection is *hijab*. The women are duty-bound to observe this degree in order to prevent corruption and deviation.

In this book, this subject has been surveyed in a number of lectures which give the reader, particularly the women, a knowledge of the Islamic view regarding *hijab*.

We wish for the dominance of human value for women in human societies, particularly Islamic societies.

International Relation Department,
Islamic Propagation Organization

CONTENTS

TRANSLATOR'S NOTE i
EDITOR'S NOTE ii

INTRODUCTION
THE WORD 'HIJAB' (MODEST DRESS) 1
THE REAL VISAGE OF THE HIJAB 5
PSYCHOLOGICAL TRANQUILITY 7
SOLIDIFYING THE ROOTS OF THE FAMILY 11
THE PERSEVERANCE OF SOCIETY 15

LESSON ONE
REASONS GIVEN FOR THE DEVELOPMENT OF THE HIJAB - PART I 17
THE PHILOSOPHICAL REASON 18
THE SOCIAL REASON 26

LESSON TWO
REASONS GIVEN FOR THE DEVELOPMENT OF HIJAB - PART II 31
THE ECONOMIC REASON 32
THE ETHICAL REASON 36
THE PSYCHOLOGICAL REASON 39

LESSON THREE
THE ISLAMIC HIJAB - PART I 49

CONTENTS

THE COMMAND TO ANNOUNCE YOUR ENTRANCE TO SOMEONE'S HOUSE 52
THE COMMAND TO 'CAST DOWN THEIR GLANCE' 58
ON THE COMMAND TO GUARD THEIR PRIVATE PARTS 60

LESSON FOUR

THE ISLAMIC HIJAB - PART II 63
THE EXCEPTIONS 64
IS 'LOOKING' PERMISSIBLE FOR MEN? 66

LESSON FIVE

THE ISLAMIC HIJAB - PART III 75
FROM THE VIEW POINT OF TRADITIONS 76
CONCERNING 'WHAT THEIR RIGHT HANDS OWN' 77
HEARING THE VOICE OF A NON-MAHRAM WOMAN 80
SHAKING HANDS 80
THESE ARE ISSUES OF RELIGIOUS EDICTS 81
MUSLIM CUSTOM 81
THE RELIGIOUS EDICTS ON THESE ISSUES 87

LESSON SIX

THE ISLAMIC HIJAB - PART IV 95
ALLOWABLE EXPEDIENCES AND NON-EXPEDIENCES 95
TRADITIONS AND NARRATIONS 100
THE EXCEPTION OF A SUITOR 102
OTHER EXCEPTIONS REFERRED TO IN THE HOLY QUR'AN 103
THE CONCLUSION OF VERSE 24:31 107

LESSON SEVEN

THE ISLAMIC HIJAB - PART V 109
SEEK PERMISSION TO ENTER ON THREE OCCASIONS 109

ON THE ISLAMIC HIJAB

"SUCH WOMEN AS ARE MENOPAUSIC..." 113

A PARTICULAR REFERENCE TO THE WIVES OF THE HOLY PROPHET 114

THE VERSE ON THE OUTER GARMENT (JILBAB) 115

EPILOGUE

THE PARTICIPATION OF WOMEN IN MEETINGS AND GATHERINGS 119

GLOSSARY 127

TRANSLATOR'S NOTE

This book, *On the Islamic Hijab*, is a translation of seven lectures delivered by Shaheed Ayatullah Murtaza Mutahhari on this topic in 1966[1] to the Islamic Physicians Association.

As it will be seen from the text of these lectures[2], this issue is presented through lively discourses in which the process of *ijtihad* (that is, strenuous endeavours to reason an issue) unfolds for those who wish to understand it.

It is the hope of all of those who endeavored to present this translation, but even more important, it was the aspiration of the one who originally presented the lectures and was martyred defending the real Islam, may Allah rest his soul in peace, that Muslim women come to understand their duties and then turn towards putting them into action so that the Islam practiced during the time of the Holy Prophet (swas) may be realized through the conduct of our Muslim women. *InshaAllah*.

Laleh Bakhtiar

---

[1] On September 30, 1966 (Mehr 8, 1345), October 14 (Mehr 22), October 28 (Aban 6), November 26 (Azar 5), December 9 (Azar 18), December 23 (Dey 2) and January 6, 1967 (Dey 16).
[2] Footnotes are elaborations from the book "*Issues on the Hijab*" by Shaheed Ayatullah Murtaza Mutahhari.

EDITOR'S NOTE

Although the contents of the text have not been altered in the translation, the sequence of the topics of the lectures has been adjusted. It is assumed that the translator has felt that the message of this presentation would be better relayed to the reader in this manner.

The reader to please keep in view that this presentation was a compilation of a series of lectures which were later published in form of book and overlook any deficiencies in this translated presentation. We have attempted with all sincerity to present the work in as accurate and comprehensive manner as possible. With the help of Almighty Allah, the reader will hopefully get the message of the one who presented these lectures and thereby benefit from it.

INTRODUCTION

THE WORD 'HIJAB'
(MODEST DRESS)

We believe in a particular philosophy in Islam for woman's *hijab* or modest dress which forms our intellectual point of view and in regard to analysis, it can be called the basis for the Islamic modest dress.

Before we begin our discussion, it is necessary to look at the meaning of the word *hijab* which is used in our age to refer to a woman's covering. This word gives the sense of 'covering' because it refers to a veil or a means of 'covering'. Perhaps it can be said that because of the origin of the word, not every covering is *hijab*. That 'covering' which is referred to as a *hijab* is that which appears behind a curtain. The Holy Qur'an describes the setting of the sun in the story of the Prophet Solomon (as)[1],

> "...until the sun was covered (bil hijab) and time for the afternoon ritual prayer was over." (38:32)

The diaphragm separating the heart from the stomach is also called *'hijab'*.

In the advice given by Imam Ali (as) to Malik Ashtar, he states,

---

[1] (as) means peace be upon him or them.

INTRODUCTION

"... prolong not your seclusion (*hijab*) from your subjects, for a ruler's seclusion from his subjects is a kind of constraint and (results in) a lack of knowledge of affairs. Seclusion from them cuts rulers off from the knowledge of that from which they have been secluded..."[2]

Ibn Khaldun says in the *Muqaddimah*, "Governments do not consider a separation to exist between themselves and the people at the beginning of their formation but little by little, the separation and distance between the ruler and the people grows and finally it causes unpleasant results."[3] Ibn Khaldun used the word *hijab* in the sense of meaning 'curtain' and 'separation' and not 'covering'.

The use of the word *satr*, in the sense of 'covering' was used instead of *hijab*, especially by the religious jurisprudents. The religious jurisprudents, whether in the section on the ritual prayers or in the section on marriage, refer to this issue and use the word *satr* and not *hijab*.

It would have been best if the word had not been changed and we had continued to use the word 'covering' or *satr* because, as we have said, the prevalent meaning of the word *hijab* is veil. If it is to be used in the sense of 'covering', it gives the idea of a woman being placed behind a curtain. This very thing has caused a great number of people to think that Islam has wanted women to always

---

[2] Letter to Malik Ashtar, the *Nahj al Balaghah*, Translated from the Arabic by William Chittick in Shi'ite Anthology. Complete text with Arabic available at: https://www.al-islam.org/nahjul-balagha-part-2-letters-and-sayings/letter-53-order-malik-al-ashtar

[3] Ibn Khaldun (1332-1406). Arab historian and forerunner of modern sociology, economics, and demography. *The Muqaddimah* is his famous work, translated from the Arabic by Franz Rosenthal.

remain behind a curtain, to be imprisoned in the house and not to leave it.

The duty for covering, which has been established for women in Islam, does not necessarily mean that they should not leave their homes. It is not the intention of Islam to imprison women. We may find such ideas in the ancient, pre-Islamic past of some countries like Iran or India but no such thing exists in Islam.

The philosophy behind the *hijab* for woman in Islam is that she should cover her body in her associations with men 'whom she is not related to according to the Divine Law' (*na-mahram*, non-*mahram*) and that she does not flaunt and display herself. The verses of the Holy Qur'an which refer to this issue affirm this and the edicts of the religious jurisprudents confirm it. We will refer to the extent of this covering by using the Qur'an and the Sunnah as sources. The relevant verses do not refer to the word *'hijab'*. Verses which refer to this issue, whether in *Surah Nur* (Chapter 24) or *Surah Ahzab* (Chapter 33), have mentioned the extent of the covering and contacts between men and women without using the word *hijab*. The verse in which the word *hijab* is used refers to the wives of the Holy Prophet of Islam (swas)[4].

We know that in the Holy Qur'an there are special commands about the Prophet's wives. The first verse addressed to them begins,
 "O wives of the Prophet! You are not as other women..." (33:32).[5]
Islam held the special relationship of the wives of the Prophet in such a great esteem that they were to remain at home for basically

---

[4] (swas) mean peace be upon him and his family (Ahlul Bayt). It is specifically used for Prophet Muhammad (swas).
[5] Also see *Sahih Muslim*, vol.4, p.148-151

INTRODUCTION

political and social reasons during the lifetime of the Holy Prophet (swas) and after his death. The Holy Qur'an says directly to the wives of the Prophet, *"Remain in your houses."* (33:33). Islam desired that the honor and respect of these 'Mothers of the Believers', who were held in great respect by the Muslims, not be misused and that they do not become a political and social tool for selfish and ambitious men.

I think that the reason why the wives of the Prophet were forbidden to marry after the Prophet's death was for this very reason. That is, a husband after the Holy Prophet (swas) might misuse the dignity and respect of his wife. Therefore, if commands are more emphatic and severe in regard to the wives of the Prophet, it is because of this.

At any rate, the verse in which the word *hijab* is used is,

"...and when you ask his wives for any object, ask them from behind a curtain (hijab)..." (33:53).

According to history and Islamic tradition, whenever you see the 'verse of *hijab*' referred to, for instance, "such and such was the case before the revelation of 'the verse of *hijab*' " or "such and such was the case after the revelation of 'the verse of *hijab*'", it refers to this verse which relates to the wives of the Prophet and not the verses of *Surah Nur* which states,

"Say to the believing men that they cast down their glance and guard their private parts. That is purer for them. Surely God is Aware of what they do. And say to the believing women that they cast down their glance..." (24: 30-31).

ON THE ISLAMIC HIJAB

Or the verse of *Surah Ahzab* which states,

"O Prophet! Say to thy wives and daughters and the believing women that they draw their outer garments (jilabib) close to them. So it is more likely that they will be known and not hurt. God is All-forgiving, All-compassionate." (33:59)

But there is a question as to why, in the recent era, the current expression of the religious jurisprudents, that is, *satr*, did not become prevalent instead of *hijab*? The reason is unknown to me. Perhaps they mistook the Islamic *hijab* for the *hijab* which is traditional in other countries. We will give further explanation about this later.

THE REAL VISAGE OF THE HIJAB

The fact is that the covering or its new expression, *hijab*, is not concerned with whether or not it is good for a woman to appear in society covered or uncovered. The point is whether or not a woman and a man's need of her should be a limitless, free association or not.

Should a man have the right to satisfy his needs with every woman and in every place short of committing adultery?

Islam, which looks at the spirit of the problem, answers: No. Men are only allowed to satisfy their sexual desires with their legal wives within a marital situation based upon the laws of marriage which establish a series of heavy commitments. It is forbidden for men to have any physical relations with women they are not related to by marriage.

INTRODUCTION

It is true that the question externally appears to be, "What should a woman do?" Must she leave her home covered or uncovered? That is, the person about whom the question is raised is a woman and the question is often expressed in very heart-rendering tones, "Is it better for a woman to be free or condemned and imprisoned in the modest dress?" But something else lies at the root of the question. That is, should men be free to take sexual benefit from women in any way they choose short of committing adultery or not? That is, the one who benefits here is a man and not a woman or at least a man benefits more than a woman does. As Will Durant has said, "The mini-skirt is a blessing for everyone in the world except cloth merchants."

So the depth of the question is whether or not the seeking of sexual pleasure should be limited to the family environment and legal wives or is the freedom of seeking sexual fulfillment something that should be satisfied in society at large? Islam defends the first theory. According to Islamic precepts, limiting sexual desires to the family environment and legal wives helps to maintain the mental health of the society. It strengthens the relationships between the members of the family and fosters the development of a perfect harmony between a husband and wife. As far as society is concerned, it keeps and preserves energies to be then used for social activities and it causes a woman to attain a higher position in the eyes of man.

The philosophy of the Islamic 'covering' depends on several things. Some of them are psychological and some relate to the home and the family. Others have sociological roots and some of them relate to raising the dignity of a woman and preventing her debasement.

ON THE ISLAMIC HIJAB

The modest dress in Islam is rooted in a more general and basic issue. That is, Islamic precepts aim at limiting all kinds of sexual enjoyment to the family and the marital environment within the bounds of marriage so that society is only a place for work and activity. It is opposite of the Western system of the present era which mixes work with sexual enjoyment. Islam separates these two environments completely.

PSYCHOLOGICAL TRANQUILITY

Without limits being established for relations between men and women or with unlimited free associations, sexual excitement and stimulation increase and demands become unquenchable and insatiable. The sexual instinct is a powerful, deep-rooted instinct which resembles the fathomless ocean. Although one thinks that by obeying it, one will have tamed it, its rebellious nature continues to show forth. It is like a fire: the more fuel is added to it, the greater would be its flame. In order to comprehend this, two points should be noted.

Firstly, just as history recalls those who coveted wealth, who were continuously seeking to add to what they already had and however much more they gained, they were still greedy for more, it also mentions those who were covetous for sexual pleasures. In no way were they satisfied by possessing beautiful women and dominating over them. This was the situation of all of those who had *harems* and, in truth, all those who had the power to possess women.

Christensen writes about the Sassanian rulers: The women we see carved into stone at Taq-i-Bustan are only a few of the 3000 women Khosrow Parviz possessed in his *harem*. This king was never

INTRODUCTION

satisfied sexually. Whenever girls, widows or women with children were presented to him for their beauty, he would order that they be sent to his *harem*. Whenever he desired to replenish his *harem*, he would write letters to his governors wherein he would describe the perfect and beautiful women he wanted. They then would send him any women who fit his description."[6]

Stories like this are endless in history. In most recent times, this greed does not take the form of *harems* but exists in another form with the difference that today it is not necessary for a person to have the wealth and possibilities that Khosrow Parviz or Harun al-Rashid had. Today, with the blessing of contemporary culture, it is possible for a man who only has one-thousandth of the possibilities of Parviz or Harun to take advantage of women.

Secondly, have you ever considered that the desire to serenade or write love poems actually stems from in humanity? A large part of world literature is filled with love poems. In this type of literature, a man praises his beloved, asks for his needs to be satisfied by the beloved, raises the position of the beloved as he lowers his own status and suffers greatly from separation. What is this? Why does humanity not behave in the same way towards needs of others?

Have you ever seen a person who worships money or a person who is ambitious for higher material positions, writing love poems on money or on ambition? Has anyone ever written a love poem asking for bread? Why is it that people enjoy listening to or reading the love poems of others? Why is it that so many people

---

[6] Arthur Christensen (1875-1945), Danish orientalist and scholar of Iranian philology; cited from his work *L'Iran sous Les Sassanides*.

receive such pleasure from Hafiz's love poems? Is it not because each person senses that it conforms to some very deep instinct which possesses their whole being? How mistaken are those who say that the one and only reason that forms the basis for human activity is an economic one!

Human beings have developed special literary rhythmic forms to express sexual love just as they have done with spiritualties whereas no special literary rhythmic forms have been developed for things that are essentially material such as bread and water. We do not want to insinuate that all loves are sexual nor do we mean to imply that all of Hafiz's or Sa'adi's poems stem from their sexual instinct. This is something that needs to be discussed separately at another time.

But what is clear is that many of the love poems are ones written by men in devotion to women. It is sufficient for us to recognize that a man's attention towards a woman is not based on bread and water so that it can be satiated when the stomach is full. Rather, it either takes the form of greed and worship of variety and multiplicity or the form of love and love poems. We will later discuss under what conditions the state of greed and sexual covetousness is strengthened and under what conditions love and love poems assume a spiritual quality.

At any rate, Islam has placed special emphasis upon the amazing power of this fiery instinct. There are traditions which speak of the danger of a 'look', the danger of a man and woman being alone together and, finally, the danger of the instinct which unites a man and a woman.

INTRODUCTION

Islam has established ways of controlling, balancing and taming the instinct. Duties have been given to both men and women in this area. One duty which is the responsibility of both men and women relates to looking at each other.

"Say to the believing men to cast down their glance and guard their private parts..." (24:30).

And,

"Say to the believing women to cast down their glance and guard their private parts." (24:31).

In summary, the command is that a man and a woman should not fix their eyes upon each other; they should not flirt with each other; they should not look at each other with lust or with the intention of seeking sexual pleasure (unless it is within the sacred bounds of marriage).

Islam has established a particular command for a woman which is that she covers her body from a man with whom she is not *mahram*[7] and that she should not flaunt herself or put her body on display in society. She is asked not to stimulate the attention of men by any means.

The human soul readily accepts stimulation. It is great error to think that the sexual desires of humanity are limited in extent and that after a certain point, are naturally satisfied. Just as the human being, man or woman, is never satiated with wealth or position and is continuously seeking more, in the area of sexual desires, it is the

---

[7] See glossary for definition of *mahram* and non-*mahram*

same. No man is ever naturally satisfied by beauty and no woman is ever naturally satisfied by a man's attention and the conquest of his heart. Clearly the desires of the heart are never satiated.

On the other hand, unlimited demands are never fulfilled and a sense of deprivation is continuously felt. Not achieving one's desires results in psychological illnesses and complexes. Why is it that in the West psychological illnesses have increased? The reason is freedom of sexual ethics and continuous sexual stimulation through the newspapers, magazines, cinemas, theaters and official and unofficial parties and even the streets and alleys.

The reason why the Islamic command to cover is exclusive to women is because the desire to show off and display one's self is a particular trait of women. She is the hunter in the domination of the hearts of men and man is the prey, whereas man is the hunter in the domination of the body of women and she is the prey. A woman's desire to display herself comes from this essence of the hunter. It is the female instinct which, because of its particular nature, wishes to capture hearts and imprison the male. Thus, the deviation begins with the female instinct and therefore the command to cover was issued.

SOLIDIFYING THE ROOTS OF THE FAMILY

There is no doubt that anything which confirms the roots of the family and increases the perception of marital relations is good for the family unit. The greatest efforts must be made to have this happen. The opposite is also true. Anything which causes the relationship between a husband and wife to grow cold is detrimental to a family and must be struggled against.

INTRODUCTION

Finding the fulfillment of sexual desires within the family environment and within the framework of a legal marriage will strengthen the relationship between a husband and wife causing their union to become more stable.

The philosophy of the modest dress and the control of sexual desires other than with a legal wife, from the point of view of the family unit, is so that one legal partner will be the cause for the wellbeing of the other, whereas in the system of free sexual relationships, one's legal partner is psychologically considered as a competitor, someone who gets in the way of that person's 'fun' like a prison guard. As a result, the basis for the family becomes enmity and hatred.

The youth of today have fled from marriage and whenever marriage is suggested to them, they say, "It is too soon. I am still too young," or give some other excuse because of this very reason. In the past, one of the greatest desires of the young people was to get married. They were not so particular before about the blessings of Europe which introduced so many women as goods.

Marriage in the past was undertaken after a time of anticipation and wishful thinking. For this very reason, the partners saw their happiness and well-being in their partner. But today, sexual desires are so freely satisfied outside of marriage that there is no longer any reason to have the former feelings. Free relationships of girls and boys have made marriage look like a duty and a limitation to them. It then becomes necessary to speak to them about ethics, morals, etc. As some magazines suggest, it must be forced upon the young people.

ON THE ISLAMIC HIJAB

The difference between the society which limits sexual relations to the family environment and a legal marriage with a society which promotes free relationships is that marriage in the first society is the end to the anticipation and deprivation whereas in the latter, it is the beginning of deprivation and limitation. In the system of free sexual relationships, the marriage contract ends the free period of boys and girls and it obliges them to learn to be loyal to each other whereas in the Islamic system, their deprivation and anticipation is met.

The system of free relationships, in the first place, causes boys to become soldiers of fortune because of marriage and the formation of a family and not until their high, young spirits tend to become weak, do they turn to marriage. Then a girl is taken because she will bear children or clean the house or act as a maid. In the second place, it weakens the roots of the existing marriage. Instead of the marriage being based upon a pure love and deep affection where they know their partner to be the person who shares in their happiness, the reverse happens.

They look at their partner with the eyes of a competitor, as a person who prevents freedom and brings limitations. As they say, each one becomes the other's prison guard. When a boy or girl want to say, "I am married," they say instead, "I have taken on a prison guard." What does this mean? This means that before marriage they were free to go wherever they wanted to flirt.

There was no one to tell them what to do. But after marriage, these freedoms were limited. If a man goes home late one night, there will be an argument with his partner. "Where were you?" If he talks with a young girl, his wife objects. It is clear to what extent family relations become weakened and cold in such a system.

INTRODUCTION

Some people like Bertrand Russell believe that the prevention of free relationships is not just for the certainty of men in relationship to future generations because methods of birth control have been developed to solve this difficulty. Thus, the issue is not just the knowledge of who the father is. The other issue is that the purest of emotions exist between the marriage partners and the relationship should be based on unity and solidarity.

These goals can only be met when the partners close their eyes to other relationships, when the man closes his eyes to other women, when the wife is not bent on stimulating and attracting anyone but her husband and when the principle of forbidding the satisfaction of sexual desires outside of the family, even before marriage, exists.

In addition, when a woman who has progressed following Russell and people like him and in accordance with the 'new sexual ethics' still seeks her love in another in spite of having a legal husband. When she sleeps with a man who has become the love of her life, what assurance is there that she will take preventing measures with a man who is her legal husband whom she does not love and not get pregnant by the man she now loves and then claims her legal husband to be the father of the child?

It is clear that such a woman will prefer to have her child be the product of the man she now loves, not of the man who the law says is her legal husband and the only person by whom she should have children. It is natural that a man should have children by a woman who loves him and not by a woman who is forced upon him by the law. Europe has clearly shown that the statistics for illegitimate children has risen at an alarming rate despite the modern means for preventing pregnancy.

THE PERSEVERANCE OF SOCIETY

Taking sexual desires from the bounds of the family environment to society has weakened society's capacity for work and activity. Contrary to the opinion that 'the modest dress results in paralyzing half of the energy potential of the individuals of society', the lack of the modest dress and the gradual development of free relationships has caused the social force to fail.

That which has caused the paralysis of women's power and that which has imprisoned her talents is the lack of the modest dress. In Islam, there is no question of the modest dress prohibiting a woman from participating in cultural, social or economic activities. Islam neither says that a woman cannot leave her home nor does it say that she cannot seek knowledge and learning.

Rather, men and women must both learn and seek knowledge. There is no objection to women's economic activities in Islam. Islam has never wanted women to be useless and unoccupied. It has never desired that women bring up useless and indifferent children. The covering of the body, except for the face and hands, is not to prevent any kind of cultural or social or economic activity. That which paralyses the working force is the corruption of the work environment by the element of seeking the satisfaction of sexual pleasures.

If a boy and a girl study in a separate environment or in one environment where the girl covers her body and wears no makeup, do they not study better? Do they not think better and listen to the

INTRODUCTION

words of the teacher better? Or is it better when a boy sits beside a girl who has on make-up and is wearing a short skirt which barely reaches her knees?

Will men work better in an environment where the streets, offices, factories, etc., are continuously filled with women who are all wearing heavy make-up and are not covered or in an environment where these scenes do not exist? Any company or office that is serious about its work and endeavors to produce good products or services, prevents these kinds of inter-mixings. If you do not believe this, check it out yourself.

The truth is that the disgraceful lack of the modest dress in Iran (he is speaking before the victory of the Islamic Revolution) whereby we were even moving ahead of America, is a product of the corrupt Western capitalist societies. It is one of the results of the worship of money and the pursuance of sexual fulfillment that is prevalent in Western capitalism.

It is one of the means they use to manipulate human society and stimulate them by this force to become consumers of their products. If an Iranian woman only wants to put on make-up for her legal husband or only wants to get dressed up for gatherings with women, she will not be a consumer of Western products. She will not be obliged to unconsciously corrupt the morals of young boys and girls, to weaken them so that they are no longer active members of society which is to the benefit of the exploiters.

LESSON ONE

REASONS GIVEN FOR THE DEVELOPMENT OF THE HIJAB - PART I

Our discourse will center around *hijab* (or the Islamic modest dress). We will discuss the modest dress from three aspects and I think that it is best if we divide it in this way.

One discussion will be a philosophical and socio-historic one about why the modest dress appeared among people, in general, because it is not particular to Islam. It existed before Islam among many of the ancient nations and it was stronger in Sassanian Iran than in any other place. What reasons have been given for this? It is possible that some of these reasons may be correct in relation to some societies? In other words, are the causes given for the development of the modest dress true in some places? Then we have to see if the reasons they have given hold true for the modest dress in Islam as well, or whether or not Islam has other reasons. We will deduce the Islamic point of view from Islam itself.

The second discussion relates to the problems which a person may find with the modest dress, the criticisms that one may make about it and the drawbacks which are mentioned. What are these drawbacks that others mention? Does the Islamic modest dress have the same drawbacks that are mentioned for the modest dress in general? Thus, the second discussion will be devoted to criticisms.

The third area of discussion relates to the Islamic modest dress itself, its history, whether or not there was the modest dress

LESSON ONE: DEVELOPMENT OF HIJAB – PART I

during the Age of Ignorance in Arabia and Islam confirmed it, increased it or decreased it? Or did it not exist in the Age of Ignorance and Islam established it?

Then, what is the Islamic modest dress? Here we will refer to the verses and commentaries upon the Holy Qur'an and traditions from the Holy Prophet (swas) and the pure Imams. The verses referred to are in two Chapters, *Surah Nur* and *Surah Ahzab*.

THE PHILOSOPHICAL REASON

Social commentators have often presented their reasons for the appearance of the modest dress centered around the idea that even in the first principles of nature, no covering or veil has been made to come between males and females. They say that there is no instance in nature where a curtain or veil appears between the male and female sex or for the female sex to be set aside behind a curtain and to wear a covering.

It would appear that there are five reasons given for the appearance of the modest dress. The philosophical reason centers on the tendency towards asceticism and struggling with pleasures in an effort to subdue the ego. The main source for this thought is perhaps India where a barrier was created between men and women through the pursuance of asceticism because a woman is the highest form of lustful pleasure giving. If men were to mix freely with women, according to this idea, a man would mainly pursue this and his society would remain underdeveloped in other areas. Therefore, he had to struggle to conquer his own soul by denying it enjoyment of sexual pleasures.

Other things which, like women, cause lust to arise within the human being are also struggled against such as the resistance towards cleanliness or encouragement of messiness and filth. Do not think that some people chose this because of carelessness on their part or because of recklessness or lack of concern. It was rooted in a philosophy which confirmed and even extended it.

As Bertrand Russell mentions in his book, Marriage and Ethics, in the early stages of Christianity, this kind of thinking developed through St. Paul when celibacy was encouraged and moved a large number of people towards the wilderness to destroy satan. Then, he says that the Church even rose in opposition to taking a bath because the body leads to sin. The Church applauded uncleanliness and a smelly body took on the smell of sanctity. According to St. Paul, cleanliness of the body opposed cleanliness of the spirit and lice come to be considered as 'pearls of God'.[1]

Then it occurred to me that having long hair among the *faqirs* who, as you know, practiced asceticism and remained celibate from women, was for this very reason. They say that in the past, whether or not it is true, whoso ever shortened or cut the hair of the body, that person's sexual instincts were strengthened. Thus, with this reasoning, long hair would lessen sexual desires.

This idea existed in the past and perhaps it is true that if a person were to cut or shorten or shave all the hair on one's body, one would increase one's sexual desires. Then the Indians and the

---

[1] Bertrand Russell (1872-1970), British philosopher, logician, historian, writer, essayist, social critic and political activist; cited from his work *Marriage and Ethics*, p. 30.

LESSON ONE: DEVELOPMENT OF HIJAB – PART I

Sikhs who forbid the cutting of their hair could have been for this very reason because they were practicing asceticism.

Some have said that the reason why the modest dress was found in the world, in an absolute sense, was because the idea of asceticism appeared. Then they ask why asceticism was found or began to develop among people. They have mentioned two reasons for this.

First, because among the deprived class, there were people who carried on with women, had beloveds and then their beloveds were taken away from them, a kind of hatred for women suddenly developed in them, in particular, where women themselves conspired against them. Thus, a hatred developed against women. They essentially began to seek celibacy and asceticism and would propagate to the extent possible against women. This they developed as a philosophy of the priests.

The second reason given for the appearance of desire for asceticism is the opposite of the first. Persons who were very extreme in their sexual practices, an extent which even exceeded the limits of nature and persons who turned to drugs or stimulators or things so that they were continuously stimulated in one way or another, would suddenly turn away from sex. It can be seen in human nature that sometimes when one does something to an extreme limit, one then turns completely away from it, even if it were something pleasurable. If something is imposed, a revulsion towards it can develop. At the end of their lives, they develop a hatred for sexual activity. History more or less confirms this in the lives of sultans who had spent their lives in carnal pleasures and *harems*. At the end of their lives, because of the extremity of their behavior, a hatred for it developed within them. They say it produced immense exhaustion within them and created a sense of antagonism and rivalry against women.

At any rate, they say that the modest dress and the barrier between men and women were caused by the appearance of the idea of seeking asceticism. The materialists who wanted to justify asceticism and ascetic practices said that it was for one of these two reasons.

As to these two reasons, we do not say that none of these existed in the world. They could have been and these causes might have had these effects but Islam, as we will mention later, established the modest dress. It did not exist during the Age of Ignorance in Arabia. We have to see whether or not these causes have been mentioned in Islam and have been given as proof or other reasons have been given for it.

Does this precept conform with other Islamic precepts? Does the Islamic spirit of asceticism conform with the concept of asceticism which we have mentioned? We will see that Islam has never presented this point of view and, as a matter of fact, Islam has struggled greatly against this view. Even non-Muslims agree that Islam never promoted asceticism and ascetic practices. The concept that began among Hindus and extended to Christianity did not exist in Islam.

It is clear that whatever Islam brought to the concept of the modest dress this reason was not one of them. Islam has emphasized cleanliness. Rather than considering lice to be God's pearls, it said, "Cleanliness stems from faith." The Holy Prophet (swas) saw a person whose hair was disheveled, whose clothes were

LESSON ONE: DEVELOPMENT OF HIJAB – PART I

dirty and he presented a bad appearance. He said, "Pleasure and taking advantage of God's blessings is part of religion."[2]

The Holy Prophet (swas) said, "The worst servants of God are those who are dirty."[3] Imam Ali (as) said, "God is beautiful and He loves beauty."[4] Imam Sadiq (as) said, "God is beautiful and He loves His creatures to embellish themselves and reflect their beauty. The reverse is also true. He considers poverty and pseudo-poverty to be enemies. If God has given you a blessing, the effect of that blessing must be shown in your life." They asked him, "How should the blessing of God be shown?" He said, "By the clothes of a person being clean, smelling good, whitening their house with stucco, sweeping in front of their house and lighting their lamps before sunset which will add to its splendor of their home."[5]

In the oldest books we have available such as *al-Kafi*, which has been used for one thousand years, there is a section called *bab alziyye wa tajammul*. Here Islam has strongly emphasized combing the hair, keeping it short, making use of perfumes and oiling one's hair.

In order to perform their worship better and in order to gain greater spiritual pleasures, a group of Companions of the Holy Prophet (swas) left their wives and children. They fasted during the day and performed worship at night. As soon as the Holy Prophet (swas) learned of this, he prevented them from continuing, saying,

---

[2] Muhammad bin al-Ḥasan al-Hurr al-Amili (1624-1693), a prominent expert of Hadith Sciences and a famous Shi'a scholar; cited from his compilation of hadithes, *Wasa'il al-Shi'ah*, vol.1, p. 277.
[3] *Wasa'il al-Shi'ah*, vol.1, p. 277.
[4] *Wasa'il al-Shi'ah*, vol.1, p. 277.
[5] *Wasa'il al-Shi'ah*, vol.1, p. 278.

"I, who am your leader, do not do this. I fast on some days and on others, I do not. I worship a part of the night and I spend other parts of it with my wives." This group then asked the Prophet's permission to castrate themselves. The Holy Prophet (swas) did not give his permission. He said that this was forbidden in Islam.

One day three women went to the Prophet. They complained about their husbands. One said that her husband did not eat meat. Another said that her husband shunned perfume. The third said that her husband distanced himself from her. The Prophet of God suddenly became angry, threw down his cloak, left his house and went to the mosque. He went upon the *minbar* (pulpit) and cried out, "What should be done with a group of my friends who put meat, perfume and women aside? I myself eat meat. I smell perfume and I receive pleasure from my wives. Whoever objects to my methods is not from among me.[6]

The command was given to shorten the length of dress because the custom among the Arabs was to wear dresses which were so long that they swept the streets. Because of cleanliness, one of the first verses revealed to the Holy Prophet (swas) was,

"And thy garments, keep free from stain." (74:4)

Also, the encouragement to wear white clothes is, first of all, because of beauty and secondly, because of cleanliness. White clothes show off dirt sooner. This has been indicated in the traditions. When the Holy Prophet (swas) wanted to meet his Companions, he would first look in a mirror, comb his hair, and

---

[6] *Wasa'il al-Shi'ah*, vol.3, p. 14. Muhammad ibn Ya'qub Kulayni (864-941), famous Shia hadith scholar; cited from his compilation *al-Kafi*, vol. 5, p. 496.

check his appearance. He said, "God loves His servants who when they are going to see their friends make themselves ready and look beautiful."[7] That is: Wear white clothes because they are more beautiful and cleaner.

The Holy Qur'an says that the creation of means of embellishment are among the kindnesses that God shows His creatures and it severely criticizes those who deny themselves the beauties of this world. The Holy Qur'an says,

"Who has forbidden the beautiful (gifts) of God which He has produced for His servants and the things, clean and pure, (which He has provided) for sustenance?" (7:32)

Islamic traditions say that the pure Imams consistently debated with the Sufis and referring to this very verse of the Holy Qur'an, invalidated their deeds.[8]

The legitimate pleasures which spouses receive from each other are considered to be blessings in Islam, among the Divine rewards. It is perhaps difficult for foreigners to understand this concept and perhaps they reflect to themselves, "How strange that they call this filthy act, a blessing, a spiritual reward!" It is surprising for a Hindu or a Christian to realize how much spiritual reward there is in performing the ritual bath (*ghusl*) after sexual intercourse and washing away the sweat which has been created by this act.

---

[7] *Wasa'il al-Shi'ah*, vol.1, p. 280
[8] *Wasa'il al-Shi'ah*, vol.1, p. 278

ON THE ISLAMIC HIJAB

Islam has placed many limitations on the issues but within the area that has been limited, not only does it not forbid it, but it encourages it and it has even presented the kindness and compassion of women as being among the qualities upheld by God's Prophets.

There is a tradition which says, "Within the nature of the Prophets is their love of woman..."[9]

The Holy Prophet (swas) straightaway forbids the seeking of asceticism and ascetic practices at the beginning of Islam, practices which may have been in imitation of monks. What a great encouragement has been given to women. In the same way that they are encouraged to limit their contacts with men who are not their husbands, they are encouraged to adorn themselves for their husbands. A woman who does not do so is even cursed; a woman must make herself beautiful for her husband. At the same time, husbands are encouraged to cleanliness.

Hasan ibn Jahm said, 'I went to see Musa ibn Ja'far', peace be upon him, and saw that he has used (hair dye) on his hair. I said, 'Have you made use of henna?' He said, 'Yes. A man's use of henna and his dressing well increases the chastity of his wife. Some women lose their chastity because their husbands do not dress well for them."[10]

In another tradition of the Holy Prophet, one of the reasons he gives for Jewish women committing adultery was because their

---

[9] *Wasa'il al-Shi'ah,* vol.1, p. 279.
[10] *Wasa'il al-Shi'ah,* vol. 3, p.3.

husbands were so filthy that their wives sought men who were clean and well-groomed."[11]

Uthman ibn Maz'un was one of the recorders of the traditions of the Holy Prophet (swas). He wanted to put this world aside in imitation of the monks and forbid himself sexual pleasures. His wife went to the Holy Prophet (swas) and said, "O Prophet of God, Uthman fasts every day and he gets up every night for prayer." The Holy Prophet (swas) became angry and went to him. Uthman was performing his ritual prayer. The Prophet waited until his ritual prayer had ended. He then said, "O Uthman, God has not sent me to institute monasticism and asceticism. God has sent me to introduce the Divine Law which is primordial and simple and to tell people about the return to God. I perform my ritual prayers. I fast and I also have relations with my wives. Whosoever loves religion which coincides with my primordial nature must follow what I do. Marriage is one of my customs."[12]

Clearly this philosophy of asceticism cannot be attributed to Islam. This philosophy might have existed in some places in the world but it does not conform to Islam.

THE SOCIAL REASON

Another cause which has been given for the observance of the modest dress is the sense of insecurity. They say that the modest dress appeared because of the lack of security which had developed.

---

[11] *Al-Kafi*, vol. 5, p. 567.
[12] *Al-Kafi*, vol. 5, p. 494.

ON THE ISLAMIC HIJAB

There were times in history when those who had power and force held the keys to everything. If people had money, property and wealth, for instance, if aristocrats had jewels, they had to hide them so that none would know what they had because whenever it became known what so and so had, powerful persons would forcibly take it away.

People who had great wealth would hide it. They would hide it so well, even from their own children that when they died no one knew where it was. They were afraid to tell their children for fear they would tell their friends, etc. and then everyone would know what they had. The person would then die and thus everything that he had remained hidden.

Lack of security was very extensive in the past. Just as there was no security in relation to wealth and property, there was no security in relation to women either. Just as men were obliged to hide their money and their wealth, they were obliged to hide their women. History records that in Sassanian Iran, the high priests and princes would seek out and take any beautiful girl that they heard about. The idea of the modest dress then was to hide women so that no other man would come to know about her.

Will Durant in his Story of Civilization writes about the situation in ancient Iran. Count Gobineau also wrote about the modest dress, "The modest dress which presently exists in Iran basically relates to pre-Islamic Iran and not Islamic Iran."[13] He believes the difference between the modest dress in Iran and the modest dress in other places is the national character of Iranians.

---

[13] Count Gobineau (1816-1882), French diplomat and travel writer. *Three Years in Iran*.

LESSON ONE: DEVELOPMENT OF HIJAB – PART I

Thus, in ancient Iran, as history tells us, the men had no assurance with regard to their women. I read a story about the time of Anushiravan the Just who had a Major in his army and even though the major had hidden his wife, word of her beauty had spread.

One day when the Major was out of town, Anushiravan went to this wife and then he returned to his palace. The woman told her husband. The man saw that not only would he now lose his wife, but his own life as well if he tried to keep her. He let her go. Anushiravan was informed that Major so and so had divorced his wife. When he saw the Major he said, "I understand you had a beautiful garden and that you sold it. Why?" The Major said. "Your majesty, I saw footprints of a lion in the garden and I was afraid the lion would eat me." He laughed and said, "No. That lion will not be found in that garden again."

Thus, there was no security. Everyone lived in fear and because of this, they say one of the causes for the appearance of the modest dress was insecurity. Then they say that this cause no longer exists. No one takes another's wife through force. Therefore, since insecurity in this sense no longer exists, there is no reason for the modest dress. Just as people can now put their money in the bank where no one will touch it, there is security. Since security exists, there is presently no need for the modest dress.

We have to compare this with the philosophy of Islam. Was the reason Islam brought the modest dress because of this question of security? When we look at the issue, we see that neither in Islamic analyses has such an issue appeared nor does it conform with history. The modest dress did not exist among the Arab bedouins during the Age of Ignorance and, at the same time, security existed That is, at the same time that individual insecurity and aggression against women had attained the greatest extent possible in Iran and women covered themselves, this type of aggression did not exist among individuals in the tribes in Arabia. The very tribal character protected the women.

The security which did not exist among the tribes was social or group security and covering does not solve this kind of problem. When two tribes fought, they not only took the men, but the women, their children and everything else as well. Covering would not have protected the women.

In spite of the obvious differences which the Arab bedouins had with our industrialized life, it resembled our life in the sense that adultery, in particular, by married women, was rampant. But because of a certain type of democracy and lack of tyranny, no one would forcibly take the wife of another man. Yet the individual insecurity which a person in the industrialized West sensed was lacking among the bedouins.

The covering prevents the aggression of a person who lives in one place. This kind of aggression does not exist among tribes. Therefore, we cannot say that Islamic precepts established the modest dress simply to provide security.

The Islamic philosophy for covering is other than this and will be explained later. At the same time, we do not want to say that the security of a woman against the aggression of a man is not at all to be considered. We will discuss this when we refer to the verse on garments. We also do not feel that this issue is irrelevant today and that women have total security against the aggression of men. All

LESSON ONE: DEVELOPMENT OF HIJAB – PART I

one has to do is to read the newspapers about the crimes committed against women in the Western world.

LESSON TWO

REASONS GIVEN FOR THE DEVELOPMENT OF HIJAB - PART II

Our discussion will center on the issue of the modest dress (*hijab*) in Islam but as we had mentioned, we must first hold a more general discussion because the modest dress is not exclusive to Islam. That is, it is not the idea that the modest dress appeared for the first time in the world with Islam. It existed before Islam among ancient peoples other than the Arab nations. It existed in ancient India and in ancient Iran, as well. The modest dress which ancient India and Iran had was much stricter than that which Islam brought. Of course, if we take the Arabian peninsula into consideration, the Islamic modest dress was established, not imitated. That is, Islam imported the modest dress into the Arabian Peninsula but it existed in non-Arab lands throughout the world.

It is a phenomenon which existed during non-Islamic times. Philosophical, social, economic, ethical and psychological reasons have been given as the cause for the development of this phenomenon and as to how it happened that the modest dress came to appear in history among people. It is necessary to mention these reasons because they have said that these are the causes for the appearance of the modest dress and that it first appeared because of certain very particular conditions which existed in those times. Conditions whereby it was, perhaps, necessary for it to be but now that those conditions no longer exist, there is no reason for the modest dress.

LESSON TWO: THE DEVELOPMENT OF HIJAB – PART II

Thus, we have to see what the reasons mentioned are, whether or not they are the real causes or is it, as some people say that which caused the modest dress to come into being was unjust. Is it that from the very beginning the modest dress itself was imposed upon women? If this is so, they conclude that this is even more reason why it should never have come into being.

In the last discussion we mentioned two reasons, one of which was the sense of insecurity. We said that this has been mentioned as a reason for women wearing the modest dress. The other reason mentioned was the sense of asceticism, the sense of struggling against sexual urges. This is something which existed in the world, in both the East and the West. In the East, one of its largest centers was India and in the West, Greece.

THE ECONOMIC REASON

Another reason given for the modest dress is that they have said that the modest dress developed because of economics, and of course, it was to exploit women. As a result of this, it is unjust. They came and divided things this way. They said history shows that there have been four eras in the relations between men and women, including the present age.

The first age of humanity, according to this view, was a communal age with reference to sex. That is, essentially no family life existed. The second era was when men dominated over women and women were seen as their slaves and a means to serve men. The second era, then, was the era of ownership by man. The third era was the age when women arose in objection to men and the fourth era is the era of equality of rights between men and women.

The first era, the communal age, they say, relates to pre-history. The era of ownership is the longest era that history has recorded where man dominated over woman and they identify Islam as an example of this era. The third era, which is known as the era of rebellion, occurred in the second half of the 19th century. The fourth era is the one which more or less has appeared or is appearing. It is the era of seeking complete equality between men and women's rights.

It is clear that these eras were developed from what others said about economics which refers to the various eras of humanity with the first era being communal, then the feudal era, the era of capitalism and the era of communism. That which they have mentioned as to the economic causes for the appearance of the modest dress does not relate whatsoever to these economic stages mentioned by others.

These four stages expressed in this manner are all erroneous. There are no facts regarding the first era which they mention as being communal. There is no evidence that family life did not exist from the very beginning.

We do not intend to go into detail about these eras but simply to refer to the fact that they say the modest dress relates to the era when men dominated over women. If we do not accept that era, they say that it resulted from men being the mediator for women: A man hired a woman for his own purposes. He kept her in his home to do his work. He left some of his work for a woman to do for him.

This was similar to when they imprisoned slaves and prevented them from leaving to better perform the work of their

LESSON TWO: THE DEVELOPMENT OF HIJAB – PART II

master. Men saw that it would be to their advantage to put women behind a curtain and prevent their comings and goings so that they would better undertake the work of the house which had been given to them to do. Thus, men did this in order for them to have hired women from the economic point of view and to have turned them into an instrument. Otherwise there was no reason to do such a thing. Wherever the modest dress has appeared, it was accompanied by such a situation of the employing of women by men to work in the house.

Is it true that this reason existed in those places in the world where the modest dress appeared? We do not deny that perhaps in some corners of the world this situation existed. If men prevented women from leaving their home and prevented others from seeing them in whatever form, if men imprisoned women, the roots of such a cause might have been economic. However, we are discussing Islam. Islam, on the one hand, established and brought the modest dress and, on the other, very directly stated something which is among the very clear aspects of Islam which is that a man has absolutely no right to gain economically from a woman. That is, a woman has economic independence. Great emphasis has been given to this issue.

That is, a man has no right to benefit economically in anyway whatsoever from a woman. The jobs of a woman belong to her. If, within the home itself, work is given to a woman to do if she so desires. But if a woman were to say, "No. I won't do that," a man has no right to force her to do it.

A woman is free in whatever work she does. In the first place, she has a right to refuse; a man has no right to order her to do something. Secondly, if she says, "I will do this for such and such a wage," she has a right to receive a wage, in the case of nursing her child, for instance. Even though a mother has priority to nurse her own child, she still has a right to obtain a wage for it. Her priority is in the sense that if another woman wanted to nurse her child and says, "I will take 1,000 rials a month to nurse the child," the mother herself says, 'I will not take more than that," then the mother has priority to nurse the child unless the other woman, for some reason, is more suitable.

A woman has a right to work outside the home as long as it does not harm the family environment. Whatever she earns belongs to her alone, no matter what legitimate work she performs.

It must be clearly recognized, then, that Islamic precepts do not intend for the modest dress to be a means to economically exploit women. If this had been the intention, the rulings would have reflected this. For instance, the precepts would have stated that a man has the right to employ his wife in his home and a woman must wear the modest dress. Then these two things would have been connected. A system which states that a man has no right to exploit a woman but, on the other hand, that same system has established the modest dress, clearly, then, did not establish the modest dress to exploit women.

We do not think, either, that this reason was a very major one for wherever in the world the modest dress existed but some Iranians who have written against the laws of Islam have greatly stressed this point. That is, they say in order for men to be able to keep women in their homes to exploit them and to turn them into their own tools, they imprisoned them. This is one reason they have given and as we have stated, this reason in no way conforms with Islam.

LESSON TWO: THE DEVELOPMENT OF HIJAB – PART II

THE ETHICAL REASON

Another reason they have given for the appearance of the modest dress has an ethical aspect. That is, it relates to the character and nature of individual.

They say it stems from the selfishness of men and men's jealousy. A man dominated over a woman so that he could enjoy her exclusively himself; so that no other man would share with him, not only in sexual intercourse but in everything. He wanted to monopolize a woman so that the touching of her body and even the viewing of her be exclusively his privilege. That is, a type of excessive greed which existed in men caused them to present the modest dress.

Russell says just this. He says that human beings have been able, to a certain extent, to dominate over their greed for wealth in such a way that they later encouraged charity and sharing one's table with others because these related to wealth. They came to regard excessive greed as something disagreeable in human beings but they were not able to control their greed for sex in the same way. Thus, they came and changed the name of this to 'manliness' or 'zeal'.

They considered jealousy and greed under this name to be a virtue whereas if charity is good and if it is good in relation to wealth, it should be good in relation to women as well, or else it is wrong in both areas. How is it that when it comes to something that belongs to a person, it is good to be generous and liberal with it but then when it relates to women, it is evil. No, there is absolutely no difference between them. If it is good, it is good for both and if it is bad, it relates to both.

In the first place, it is not right to compare 'having a wife' to 'having property'. Secondly, from our point of view, there is a difference between jealousy and zeal (passion, fervor or ardency, *ghairat*). We believe them to be two different feelings. Zeal is a natural instinct given to humanity. It is a collective word. That is, its roots are to preserve society, not an individual. It is like a policeman that God has placed within humanity to preserve future generations.

As we have pointed out, however, much satisfaction a man receives in sexual pleasures, his sense of zeal becomes more weakened along with his sensitivities towards modesty, piety and moral will-power. Lustful men do not object to their wives having affairs; they may even enjoy it and defend such deeds.

Whereas the opposite is true of men who struggle against their ego's desires and lust. In this struggle, gathering together their moral forces, they dominate over vices such as greed, envy or the worship of money within themselves. They become what the term 'human being' really means. They then devote themselves to serving people as a sense of providing service to others develops within them. Such men have greater 'zeal' or 'sense of manliness' and are more jealous and protective of women. As a matter of fact, they protect all women in general. That is, their conscience does not permit them to allow any kind of aggression against women in society for it is as if they were the protectors of all women.

Imam Ali (as) said, "A noble, zealous person never commits adultery." He did not say 'a jealous person never commits adultery' but rather a zealous one. Why? Because manliness is a noble human virtue. It is a human virtue which relates to society and its purity. Just as a zealous man does not allow the corruption of women he is related to, neither is he content to see the women of society being corrupted. This is because zeal is other than jealousy. Jealousy is a personal and individual affair and stems from a series of spiritual beliefs but zeal is an emotion and a sensitivity which relates to the human species as a whole.

The secret of the fact that men have a very great sensitivity towards their wife having sexual intercourse with other men is an instinct which creation gave to every man to preserve future generations. If this did not exist, if the singular affection for children did not exist, not even one individual would be inclined towards reproduction. If this sense of wonder did not exist within the human being to protect and guard the place of the seed so that other seeds, which are similar, would not fall there, the relation between the sexes would be completely cut off. No one would know their father and no father would know his child whereas the connection between one generation to another is one of the principles of human society. If it did not exist, there would be no society.

Human beings have been given an instinct which is the basis for the preservation of society and that instinct is this: Women are desirous of preserving their generations and so are men but women are protected as a result. When a child is born, it is clear who its mother is and the mother knows her child. Even if she were to have intercourse with a thousand men, she would know that the future generations are assured but men are not reassured in this way unless they have guarded that woman and created some precautions whereby they are assured of their fatherhood.

Can a person say that we must eliminate this instinct called 'zeal' which exists within human beings? And, that this is the same thing as jealousy? This is something which even those who have a community type of living as far as property is concerned have not said in relation to women.

THE PSYCHOLOGICAL REASON

Some people believe that the modest dress and staying at home are based on psychological reasons and that women have had an inferiority complex towards men from the very beginning. This feeling is based on two reasons: One is that some women think they lack something organic in their body in comparison to men. The other reason is the bleeding during their monthly menstruation and following childbirth.

The monthly period was considered to be a kind of deficiency in ancient times. That is why women were isolated during their monthly period and everybody avoided associating with them.

Perhaps that was the main reason for asking the Holy Prophet (swas) a question on this subject. God revealed a special verse in answer to this question. The Qur'an does not say that menstruation is something deplorable and that a woman is to be isolated during this time and that no one should associate with her.

It says that it is a kind of harm leaving the body and during this time, they should not have sexual intercourse. It does not say that they should not associate with each other.

"They ask you about menstruation. Say: It is a kind of harm. Do not have sexual intercourse with women at this time." (2:222)

LESSON TWO: THE DEVELOPMENT OF HIJAB – PART II

According to the Qur'an, it is a kind of harm like many others and it is far from being deplorable.

Abu Dawud related a Tradition of the Holy Prophet (swas): "Ibn Malik said that the Jewish people used to send their wives out of their home when they were menstruating. They did not eat with them and did not drink water from their glass. They did not remain in the same room with them either. For this reason, the Prophet was asked about this and the above verse descended. The Prophet forbade the isolation of women at this time and said, 'Nothing is forbidden except sexual intercourse.'[1]

According to Islam, the menstruating woman is *muhdis*, that is, a person who does not perform the partial or total ritual ablution. Such a person is deprived from performing the ritual prayer and fasting. Every *hadas* is a kind of ritual impurity which is removed by ritual purification such as a partial or total ablution. By this we mean that the state of menstruation is like the state of having had a wet dream or sexual intercourse, etc. But this ritual state is not special for women and it is removed by partial or total ritual ablution.

Many ideas have been expressed about the fact that women have a sort of deficiency in their feelings and because of this, both men and women thought that women were abased. Whether they are correct or incorrect, there is no relation between this and the philosophy of Islam about women and the modest dress or 'covering'. Islamic precepts neither refer to menstruation nor the modest dress as reasons to consider women lowly or abased.

---

[1] *Sunnan Abi Dawud*, Chapter *Al-Haid* (the menstruating women), p.102.

These, then, are the five causes which others have more or less related and from none of the five which are mentioned is one able to say that the modest dress is no longer necessary or that it was unjust from the very beginning.

Can the modest dress have another cause or not? May we offer the fact that the modest dress in Islam has other reasons which do not compare to any of these five reasons mentioned: the well-being of a person's 'self', family and society.

It is well known that the spirit of the human being, just like a person's body, can either be healthy or sick. What is the cause for its sickness? They have given many reasons. One of the reasons mentioned is frustration, the failure to attain one's desires, deprivation or disillusionment.

Some people have suggested that these sexual frustrations arise from social limitations. With the removal of these limitations, all individuals will then succeed in the area of sexual affairs and sexual frustrations will disappear. This assumption was put forward but the drawbacks to it became quite apparent. It became clear that although it is true that sexual frustration causes psychological illnesses, it cannot be eliminated by the removal of the limits because if we remove social limits, we will only serve to further stimulate sexual urges, thereby increasing demands which only lead to further disillusionment within the human being.

For instance, say that a human being had a limited number of demands, such as the demands in relation to food. Every society has a certain amount of demand for food. If a country has a population of 20 million, the amount of food required is clear. If their supply is

LESSON TWO: THE DEVELOPMENT OF HIJAB – PART II

greater than that, they cannot consume it. It should not be less but if it is more, they have to throw it away.

When demands are limited, they can be satisfied. Demands can even be decreased in relation to the supply but it has been proven that the demand of certain things in human beings are unlimited. However much they are satisfied, the desire persists. Things which have a quality which are not solely physical are like this. For instance, in the area of material things, if we want to say how much food a society needs, we can estimate this but if we were to ask how much money a society needed, the demand would be unlimited.

We may ask, "How much wheat would it take to satisfy the people of Iran?" This is possible to estimate. But it is more difficult to estimate if we ask, "How much money would satisfy the people of the country?" If you give as much as possible to an individual, he would never say: That's enough. Knowledge is also like this.

Many of the demands of human beings are rooted in unending human desires. When you relate to them, a person still says: I want more. Wealth is also like this. It cannot be satiated. A tradition of the Holy Prophet (swas) relates to this. "There are two kinds of hunger which are never fulfilled, the hunger for knowledge and the hunger for wealth."[2]

Can one fulfil the ambition of a person? Can a society fulfil the ambition of a person? No. No matter what position a person is given, that person wants an even higher position. Even if you gave him the highest position, he still would not be satisfied. The reason

---

[2] *Sunan al-Daremi*, Moqaddamah, p.32

for the development of ethics was because of this very thing, that is, to regulate unending human desires which have created chaos and conflicts.

Sexual enjoyment is limited from the physical point of view. A man can be satisfied from one woman, or, at the most, two. But from the point of view of attachment that a man and a woman develop, even Russell mentions the fact that physical sex differs from the attachment which can result from it. When it takes on this quality, can it be fulfilled? Given a man who has fallen into this way, a man, for instance, who has a *harem* of a thousand beautiful women. If someone were to say to him, "There is a beautiful woman in such and such a place", would he then say, "No. I am satisfied with my *harem* and my relations with the women there." There is no question of ever being satiated.

It was because of this that they readily saw that the desire for sex is like wealth. It is insatiable. They came and gave another suggestion. The human being must be made to deviate from this way. A person must be placed upon the unending road, a road that leads nowhere. Freud suggested it. He first struggled against any kind of social limits and limitations. He then saw that giving people limitless sexual freedom created more difficulties and problems for them. It created far greater psychological disturbances. He said, "This spirit must be directed to other things so that it becomes preoccupied with art, literature, etc. because this way is impossible!" This spirit has to be allowed to develop without anything standing in its way.

Experience and statistics have shown that in the West where sexual freedom is very great and in some areas, there are no limitations, psychological illnesses are greater than in a society

LESSON TWO: THE DEVELOPMENT OF HIJAB – PART II

which has limitations. The greater the stimulation, the more the desires increase. They increase several times just like fire. Can a person satiate a fire with fuel? This clearly cannot be done.

They say that no matter how you try to prevent a human being from something, the greed for it increases. This is true but the point to note is that the human being develops greed for something which is both forbidden and stimulated but if it is not offered or it is offered less, the human being finds less desire for it. When it is stimulated it is impossible for everyone to satisfy their desires for it no matter how much freedom they are given.

Thus, if there is a kind of limitation and sexual desires are to be satisfied within the marital environment, if society is to be the place of work and activity, if a woman does not have the right to stimulate sexual urges nor a man have the right to seek sexual fulfillment outside the marital environment, if it takes this form, the spirit and morale of people will clearly develop in a more healthy and wholesome way.

As to the family, efforts must be made so that, to the extent possible, marital relations become more and more intimate and whatever will weaken this relationship must be resisted. The limiting of sexual fulfillment to marriage, whatever kind of fulfillment it may be, causes the married couple to develop a more profound union because a man and a woman who knows only her husband to be the source of her pleasure and happiness clearly will develop deeper and stronger ties.

For instance, some people ask why it is that sexual relations of a man without a wife and a woman without a husband are forbidden outside of marriage? Why can they not have sexual relations? We accept the fact that there is a difference but note this point which appears to be very clear to me. In the recent past and in the present among societies which live according to Islamic law, a girl who reaches puberty is not free to take sexual enjoyment from every youth even though the instinctive desire exists.

When a boy reaches puberty, a desire and inclination for the opposite sex develops but there are no means to satiate it.

From the beginning he is told, for instance, that he can marry when he reaches the age of 20 and the girl knows that he will marry in a few years. Marriage for them is a very sweet and pleasurable thing. Marriage is a fulfillment of desires after a time of deprivation. That is, sexual urges may not be satisfied outside of marriage.

This boy who is facing a girl for the first time sees her as the person who will satisfy his desires, bring him pleasure and happiness and the girl who faces the boy for the first time, knowing he will bring her happiness and well-being, develop such emotions that are incomparable to anything else.

Marriage and the family center are like this. When the satisfaction of sexual urges is forbidden outside this realm, it becomes the center of happiness.

Thus this issue of forbidding the fulfillment of sexual activities outside of the family center serves to strengthen family solidarity whereas allowing such possibilities outside the family center separates the family. As we will come to point out, the Islamic modest dress is nothing more than this; the limiting or restricting the sexual needs to marriage.

LESSON TWO: THE DEVELOPMENT OF HIJAB – PART II

Now we will look at society. It has been said that the modest dress paralyzes half of the society. I accept that if the modest dress were that which they say existed among the Indians or that which existed in ancient Iran, this may be true.

But the Islamic modest dress does not say that a woman should be imprisoned nor does it say that a woman has no right to leave her home or to do a particular job which is of a social or economic nature. Islamic precepts say, as we will read in the verses of the Holy Qur'an and in the Traditions, that a woman who leaves her home does not have the right to leave in such a way that she stimulates other men or attracts them towards herself. This is a particular duty of women. And no man has the right to cast a lustful look towards a woman who leaves her home. This is a particular duty of men.

If a woman did not speak in stimulating tones in a social situation, if this did not happen, would boys and girls not study better? If boys did not have the right to flirt, would society not function better? If a woman is wearing the modest dress and goes to buy something and the seller knows that this is not the place for games, which way is better? Clearly if there is the Islamic modest dress, the human task force will most certainly perform with more efficiency and in this manner, work productivity will improve.

That which has been created clearly prevents work from progressing as it should. Students do not study; marketing has been made to deviate from its main purpose which is selling quality goods. Instead they empty the pockets of people by showing a beautiful woman who is selling something. Men go to buy, not caring what the product is, to enable them to talk to her. Will this cause society to deviate?

Thus, from the point of view of work and social activity, the improvement of society dictates that it should not be the place for the stimulation or fulfillment of sexual urges and the Islamic modest dress serves just this purpose.

LESSON THREE

THE ISLAMIC HIJAB - PART I
THE HIJAB BRINGS DIGNITY TO A WOMAN

There is one issue which remains to be discussed. It is one of the criticism they have made against the modest dress which says that the modest dress deprives the honor and respect of a woman. You know that human dignity has become one of the important goals of humanity since the words about human rights have developed. Human dignity is respected and it must be followed; all human beings share in this whether man or woman, black or white, or whatever nation or creed. Every individual has this right to human dignity.

They say that the Islamic modest dress opposes a woman's dignity. We accept the right of human dignity. The discussion is whether or not the modest dress, i.e., the modest dress which Islamic precepts mention, is disrespectful to women, an insult to her dignity. This idea came into being from the idea that the modest dress imprisons a woman, making her a slave.

Enslavement opposes human dignity. They say because the modest dress was introduced by men to enable them to exploit women, men wanted to captivate woman and imprison her in a corner of her home. Thus, it is to have overlooked or insulted her human dignity. Respect, honor and nobility of a woman call for not having a modest dress.

LESSON THREE: THE ISLAMIC HIJAB – PART I

As we have said and we will further describe later, that is, we will deduce from the verses of the Holy Qur'an that we have nothing which would serve to imprison a woman and the necessities of the Islamic modest dress are not to imprison a woman. If a man has duties in his relation to a woman or a woman has duties in relation to a man, the duty is in order to strengthen and solidify the family unit. That is, it has a clear purpose.

In addition, from the social point of view, it has necessities. That is, the well-being of society demands that a man and a woman commit themselves to a special kind of association with each other or the ethical sanctities and ethical balance and the tranquility of the spirit of society, demand that a man and a woman choose a special way of relating to each other. This is neither called imprisonment nor enslavement nor does it oppose human dignity.

As we observe if a man leaves his house naked, he is blamed and reproached and perhaps the police will arrest him. That is, even if a man leaves his house with pajamas on, or with just underpants, everyone will stop him because it opposes social dignity. Law or custom rules that when a man leaves the house, he should be covered and fully dressed. Does this oppose human dignity to tell him to cover himself and leave the house?

On the other hand, if a woman leaves her house covered within the limits that we will later mention, it causes greater respect for her. That is, it prevents the interference of men who lack morality and ethics. It a woman leaves her house covered, not only does it not detract from her human dignity, but it adds to it. Take a woman who leaves her home with only her face and two hands showing and from her behavior and the clothes she wears there is nothing which would cause others to be stimulated or attracted

ON THE ISLAMIC HIJAB

towards her. That is, she does not invite men to herself. She does not wear clothes that speak out or walk in a way to draw attention to herself or does not speak in such a way to attract attention.

Sometimes the clothes of an individual speak. His or her shoes speak. The way she or he talks says something else. Take a man, for instance, who speaks in such a way so as to say, "Fear me," or dresses in such a way opposite to that which is customary. That is, with a traditional cloak, a beard and a turban, etc., communicates to the people, "Respect me."

It is possible that a woman wears clothes in such a manner that a human being, a respected human being, would associate among people and it is possible that she wears clothes and walks in a way which stimulates; "Come and follow me." Does the dignity of a woman, the dignity of a man, or the dignity of society not cause a woman to leave her home serious, diligent and simply dressed in a manner not drawing the attention of everyone she passes by.

She should be such that she does not distract a man and turn his attention from what he is doing. Does this oppose a woman's dignity? Or does it oppose the dignity of society? If a person says something, which existed in non-Islamic societies, that the modest dress was to imprison women, that a woman must be placed in a locked house and she should have no right of association outside the home, this does not relate to Islam. If Islamic precepts were to say that it is not permitted for a woman to leave her house; if we were to ask whether it is possible for a woman to buy something from a store where the seller be a man and they said no, it was forbidden; if a person asked, "Is a woman permitted to participate in meetings, religious gatherings?" and we were to say no, it is not permitted; if it is possible for women to meet each other?; if

51

LESSON THREE: THE ISLAMIC HIJAB – PART I

someone were to say all of these were forbidden, that a woman must sit in a corner of the house and never leave her home, this would be something, but Islam does not state this.

We say this is based on two things. One is based upon that which is good for the family. That is, a woman must not do anything that would disturb her family situation. For a woman to leave her house to go to her sister's house if her sister is a corrupt and licentious person or even to visit her mother wherein the effects of the visit bring chaos to the house for a week, they say not to under such circumstances. The family must not be disturbed.

The second basis is that leaving the house, according to the Holy Qur'an, must not be in order to flaunt oneself, to disturb the peace and tranquility of others, to prevent the work of others. If it is not these things, there is no problem.

THE COMMAND TO ANNOUNCE YOUR ENTRANCE TO SOMEONE'S HOUSE

Now we will discuss the Qur'anic verses and after we clarify what traditional commentators have explained about the verses, then, with the help of traditions which have been narrated on this topic and the edicts of the religious jurisprudents on this issue, it will become clearer. The verses relating to the modest dress are found in *Surah Nur* and *Surah Ahzab*. We will mention all of them.

We will begin our discussion with the verses from *Surah Nur*. Of course the verses which relate directly to the modest dress are verses 30 and 31 of *Surah Nur* but there are three verses before this which are more or less introductory to the modest dress and relate to this issue.

"O you who believe! Do not enter houses other than your own houses until you have asked permission and saluted their inmates; this is better for you, that you may be mindful." (24:27)

This verse describes the duty of a man who is not *mahram*, to the house of another person, that is, the house of a person whose wife is not *mahram* to him. Of course, there are rules regarding those who are *mahram* and we will mention them later. Also there are some places where it is not particular to those who are *mahram*. It relates to what a person who wants to enter the house of another should do.

To begin with, let me say that during the Age of Ignorance before the Holy Qur'an was revealed, the present situation of houses did not exist with locks, etc. Doors are closed basically because of the fear of thieves. If someone wanted to enter, he would ring the doorbell or use the knocker. In the Age of Ignorance this situation did not exist. It was more like the situation in villages. People like myself who lived in the village know that there were basically no doors shut. The doors to the courtyard are always open. In many places it is not even the practice to lock the doors at night. In Fariman, a town near Mashhad, where I lived, I do not remember the door to the yard being closed even once and there was very little theft.

History shows that, in particular in Makkah, they often did not even put doors on a house. In Islam a law was passed that a person never owns their house in Makkah. Of course, there is a difference of opinion among the religious jurisprudents. The Imamis (Shias) and the Shafiis agree that in Makkah, the land cannot belong to any one person. That is, it belongs to all Muslims and the land of

LESSON THREE: THE ISLAMIC HIJAB – PART I

Makkah cannot be bought and sold. The houses belong to all the people. It has the ruling of a mosque. In *Surah Hajj* it says that the people who live there and the people who come from outside that area are all the same.

These rents which people collect today in Makkah neither agrees with the Shi'ite jurisprudence nor with much of the Sunni jurisprudence. It must have an international ruling. They have no right to establish limits there and not allow a person to enter. It is like the room in a mosque, everyone can have a room there. It belongs to him but he has no right to prevent others from entering. The person has no right to close off an empty room. Of course, if a person is using it, he has priority.

The first person who gave the order for doors to be placed on the houses was Mu'awiyah. This had been forbidden to be done to the houses of Makkah. This was the general situation.

It was not the custom among Arabs in the Age of Ignorance to announce that they wanted permission to enter. They felt it was an insult to seek permission to enter. The Holy Qur'an says in another verse, "If you go and seek permission and it is not granted, return."

This may be considered to be an insult by some but this emphasis in the Holy Qur'an is one of the introductory aspects of the modest dress because every woman in her own home is in a situation that she does not want to be seen or she does not want to see a person. A verse was revealed.

"And when you ask his wives for something, ask them from behind a curtain (hijab)." (33:53)

Thus, a person must first seek permission to enter and then, with the agreement of the owners, the person enters even if the other party knows that he wants to enter.

The Holy Prophet (swas) said: "In order to announce your entrance, recall God's name in a loud voice." I later realized the words 'ya Allah' that Muslims say, for instance, to enter, is the implementation of this command.

Thus, announce and how much better it is when this announcement is made by the recitation of God's name. The Holy Prophet (swas) continuously did this and he was asked, "Is this a general ruling that we should use when we enter our sister's house, our daughters house, our mothers house?" He said, "If your mother is getting undressed, would she want you to see her then?" They said, "No." He said, "Then this same ruling holds for one's mothers house. Do not enter without announcing your entrance."

When the Holy Prophet (swas) would enter, he would stand behind the door of the room in a place where they could hear his voice and would call out, "*As-salam alaykum ya ahl al-bayt*" ("Peace be upon you oh household of the Prophet"). He said, "If you hear no answer, perhaps the person did not hear you. Repeat it again in a loud voice. Repeat for a third time if you receive no response. If, after the third time that you announce yourself, you hear no response, either that person is not home or the person does not want you to enter; return." The Holy Prophet (swas) did this and many stories have been narrated about this, such as when he wanted to enter his daughter's house, he would call out salutations in a loud voice. If she responded, he would enter. If he called out three times and received no response, he would return.

LESSON THREE: THE ISLAMIC HIJAB – PART I

There is something here to note which is the difference between *dar* and *bayt* in Arabic. *Dar* is that which we call courtyard. They call a room, *bayt*. The Holy Qur'an refers to *bayt*, that is, when you want to enter the room of a person. Since the doors to the courtyards were open, the courtyard clearly did not assume an area of privacy. That is, if a woman was dressed in such a way that she did not want anyone to see her, she would not be so dressed in the courtyard. She would go into a room. The courtyard has the ruling of a room. The door is closed and it normally has high walls. Women still consider the courtyard to be, to a certain extent, a place of privacy. Now *dar* has the ruling of *bayt* because *bayt* basically means the place of privacy where a woman does not want a strange person to see her.

"This is purer for you." That is, the commands We give are better for you, contain goodness, are not illogical. "Know that this is good."

"O you who have faith! Do not enter houses other than your own until you have announced [your arrival] and greeted their occupants. That is better for you. Maybe you will take admonition." (24:27)

"But if you do not find anyone in them, do not enter them until you are given permission. And if you are told: 'Turn back,' then do turn back. That is more decent for you. Allah knows best what you do." (24:28)

This was very difficult for the Arabs to understand. To seek permission when they wanted to enter a house was itself difficult and then to be told to return and then to actually do so, was next to impossible. It was an insult.

In the verse, "*That is more decent for you...*", an exception arises. Does this ruling apply whenever one wants to enter anyone's home or only a person's residence? The Holy Qur'an says this is not a general ruling and only applies to someone's home.

A home is a place of privacy, the place of one's private life. If this were not so, there would be need to seek permission. If there is, for instance, a caravanserai and you have business, do you have to seek permission, etc? No. Here it is not necessary to enter by seeking permission. What about a public bath? There is no need here. "*That is more decent for you...*" if it is not a place of residence in which you have business. "*God knows what you reveal and what you hide.*"

From the word, 'uninhabited', one can understand that the philosophy of why a person cannot enter the home of another without announcing it first is because of the wife as well as the fact that the home is the place of one's privacy. Perhaps there are things which one does not want someone else to see.

Thus, when a person enters the privacy of another's home, the entrance must be announced. A person must, in some way, announce that he wants to enter even if the person knows that the other has allowed him to enter. He is your friend. He knows that you are going to enter. You know that he is totally in agreement with your entering. Still, you should realize that you are entering upon his privacy.

LESSON THREE: THE ISLAMIC HIJAB – PART I

THE COMMAND TO 'CAST DOWN THEIR GLANCE'

"*Say to the believing men that they cast down their glance and guard their private parts; that is purer for them. God is aware of the things they do.*" (24:30)

"*Say to the believing women that they cast down their glance and guard their private parts and reveal not their adornment except such as is outward and let them cast their veils (khumar) over their bosoms and reveal not their adornment except to their husbands, their fathers, or their husbands' fathers or their sons or their husbands' sons, or their brothers or their brothers' sons, or their sisters' sons or their women or what their right hands own, or such men as attend to them, not having sexual desire, or children who have not yet attained knowledge of women's private parts nor let them stamp their feet, so that their hidden ornament may be known. And turn all together to God, O you believers, so you will prosper.*" (24:31)

In the phrase, "*Say to the believing men that they cast down their glance,*" there are two words which we have to define. One is *ghadh* and the other is *absar*. A person who might say *absar*, the plural of *basar*, needs no explanation because it means eyes but *absar* essentially means 'sight'. If it had said '*ain asin ghamdh'ain* it would have meant 'close their eyes'. It would have had a particular meaning in this case. What does *ghadh basar* mean? *Ghadh* means 'lower', 'cast down', not 'cover' or 'close'. We see this in another verse,
"*Be modest in your bearing, and lower (yaghaddwu) your voice. Indeed the ungainliest of voices is the donkey's voice.*" (31:19)

This does not mean to be silent. A person's voice should be moderate. In the same way, 'to cast down one's glance' means not to look in a fixed way, not to stare.

In a famous tradition of Hind ibn Abi Halah which describes the Holy Prophet (swas), it is recorded, "When he was happy, he would cast down his glance."[1] It is clear it does not mean he closed his eyes.

Majlisi in Bihar interprets the sentence about the Holy Prophet (swas) thus: "He would cover his gaze and put down his head. He did this so that his happiness would not show."

Imam 'Ali (as) in the *Nahj al-Balaghah* says to his son Imam Hasan (as), when he gave a banner to him in the Battle of Jamal 'Even if the mountains are uprooted, do not leave your place. Clench your teeth (so that your anger increases). Bare your head to God. Nail your feet to the ground. Survey the enemy's forces and cast down your glance."[2] That is, 'do not fix your gaze on the enemy.'

There are essentially two ways of looking. One is to look at another with care as if you were evaluating the person by the way he looked or dressed. But another kind of looking is in order to speak to that person and you look since looking is necessary for conversation. This is a looking which is introductory and a means for speaking. This is an organic looking while the former is an autonomous kind. Thus, the sentence means: "Tell the believers not to stare at or flirt with women."

---

[1] *Tafsir ul Quran*, Safi, 24:31, narrated from a tradition of 'Ali ibn Ibrahim Qummi

[2] *Nahj al Balaghah*, Sermon 110.

LESSON THREE: THE ISLAMIC HIJAB – PART I

ON THE COMMAND TO GUARD THEIR PRIVATE PARTS

In the next sentence it says,

"Tell the believing men. . . to guard their private parts." (24:30)

To guard from what? From everything which is not correct, guard against both corruption and the glance of others.

As you know, it was not the custom among Arabs in the Age of Ignorance to hide their private parts. Islam came and made it obligatory to cover this area.

It should be noted that the present Western civilization is moving directly towards the habits of the pre-Islamic Arabs in the Age of Ignorance and they are continuously weaving philosophies justifying that nakedness is a good thing. Russell in "On Discipline," says that another illogical ethics or taboo is that a mother and father tell their children to cover themselves which only creates a greater curiosity in children and parents should show their sexual organs to children so that they become aware of whatever there is from the beginning. Now, they do this.

But the Holy Qur'an says, **"And guard their private parts,"** both from corruption and from the view of others. Covering one's private parts is obligatory in Islam except, of course, between a husband and wife and it is among the most disapproved acts for a mother to be naked before her son or a father before his daughter.

"That is purer for them. God is aware of the things they do." (24:30).

ON THE ISLAMIC HIJAB

The Holy Prophet (swas) said from his childhood a certain event occurred several times. He sensed that there was another kind of power within him and it would not allow him to do things that were being done during the Age of Ignorance. He said once when he was a child he was playing with the children. Masons were building a house for one the Quraish nearby. The children enjoyed helping the builders by bringing then stones, bricks, etc. The children would carry them in their long white skirts (underneath which they wore nothing) and then place them before the builders. In doing so, their private parts would be revealed. The Holy Prophet (swas) related that he went and put a stone in the skirt of his long chemise and when he wanted to rise, something stopped him and hit against the skirt of his dress. He repeated it and he had the same feeling. He then realized that he should not do this and he did not try it again.[3]

"Say to the believing women that they cast down their glance..." (24:31) You see that in these two verses, the ruling for a man and woman is the same. This is not something particular to men. For instance, if women were forbidden from looking and not men, there would have been a distinction that such and such was all right for men but not for women. It is clear, then, that when there is no distinction made between men and women, it has another purpose which we shall discuss in the next lesson.

---

[3] Ibn Abi al-Hadid, *Sharhe Nahjul Balaghah*, Sermon 190

LESSON FOUR

THE ISLAMIC HIJAB - PART II
THE COMMAND "NOT TO REVEAL THEIR ADORNMENT"
AND
"TO GUARD THEIR PRIVATE PARTS"

The word *farj* is used in Arabic to refer to both a man and a woman's private parts. The fact that men and women have both been commanded to guard their modesty, to guard their private parts is in relation to two things: the view of others and this includes everybody except a husband and wife, and the other is that one should guard one's modesty from corruption, from adultery. If we look at the external form of the verse, perhaps we would conclude that it only refers to corruption but because, from the time of the Prophet's Companions and the very first commentaries on the Holy Qur'an, it has been clearly recorded that wherever the Holy Qur'an says, "*guard their private parts,*" it means from adultery except in those verses where it is to guard the private parts from the view of others. Thus, this verse, either refers to the collective view or it refers to the view of others if we take the traditions into account. There is no difference of opinion here.

The third duty is not to reveal "*their adornment...*" which refers to that which is separate from the body like jewels and gold as well as things that are attached to the body like henna or collyrium.

LESSON FOUR: THE ISLAMIC HIJAB – PART II

THE EXCEPTIONS

As to the fact that they should *"reveal not their adornment,"* there are two exceptions in the Holy Qur'an. The first is *"except such as is outward"* and the second is *"except to their husbands...etc."* Both of these have to be discussed further, in particular, the first exception.

Women should *"not reveal their adornment... except such as is outward."* What does this refer to? Is it beauty which is most often hidden under clothes that must not be revealed? Then what is that which "is outward?" From the beginning of Islam, many questions arose in relation to *"except such as is outward"* which were asked from the Companions of the Holy Prophet (swas) and the Helpers and many Shi'ites asked the pure Imams. There is almost total agreement regarding this point. That is, whether one is a Sunni who refers to the Companions and Helpers of the Holy Prophet (swas) or one be a Shi'ite who refers to the recorders of those traditions, there is more or less agreement that which "is outward" is collyrium, a ring and, in some, an anklet.

That is, adornments which are used on the two hands and the face. This then shows that it is not obligatory for women to cover their face or their hands. Things which adorn them may appear as long as they are part of common usage. The adornments which are applied to the hands and the face are not obligatory to be covered.

There are great many traditions in relation to this. It was asked from Imam Sadiq (as) what may be displayed of adornments. That is, those things which are not obligatory to cover. He said, "It refers to collyrium and a ring and they are on the face and hands."[1] Abi Basir said he asked Imam Sadiq (as) about the exception and he said a ring and bracelet."[2]

There is a tradition recorded by a person who was not a Shi'ite but because of his reliability, he is referred to and quoted by the *'ulama*. He says that he heard from Imam Ja'far Sadiq (as), upon him, that the exception is the face and the hands. These are all similar in what they say. When the face and hands do not need to be covered, then their adornment, even more so.

There is another tradition narrated by Ali ibn Ibrahim from Imam Baqir (as). He was asked about this exception and he said it includes a woman's clothes, collyrium, ring and coloring of the palms of the hands and a bracelet."[3] Then the Imam (as) said that we have three levels of adornment, the adornment all people may see, the adornment which *mahram* may see and the adornment for one's spouse. That which may be displayed for the people is the face and hands and their adornment such as collyrium, a ring, a bracelet but the adornment which may be displayed before someone who is *mahram* is the neck and above including a necklace, an armlet, hands plus an anklet and anything below the ankles.

There is, of course, a difference of opinion as to what can be revealed before someone who is *mahram*. That which can be concluded from the totality of the traditions and according to the edicts of the religious jurisprudents is that no one is *mahram* other than one's husband from the navel to the knees. That is, a woman

---

[1] *Al-Kafi*, vol. 5, p. 521 and *Wasail al-Shiah*, vol. 3, p. 25.
[2] *Ibid.*
[3] *Tafsir ul Quran*, Safi, 24:31.

LESSON FOUR: THE ISLAMIC HIJAB – PART II

must cover herself from the navel to the knee from even her father or brother and from the navel above, it must be covered from everyone except one's father. But for the husband, a woman may display her whole body.

We have other traditions in this area as well such as the fact that women must 'cast their veils over their bosoms'. Before the revelation of this verse, women would wear a scarf but they would place the ends behind their head so that their earrings, neck and chest would show since their dresses were most often v-necked. With the revelation of this verse, it became clear that they had to cover their ears, neck and chest with their head covering. There is a traditional recorded by Ibn Abbas, the well-known transmitter of traditions, that it is obligatory for women to cover their chests and neck.[4]

The first exception we have referred to relates to what is not obligatory to be covered. The second exception refers to those before whom it is not obligatory to cover such as fathers, husbands, children, etc.

IS 'LOOKING' PERMISSIBLE FOR MEN?

In this area there are two points to be recognized and separated, at least mentally. One is what is obligatory for women to cover and what is not. If we say that it is not obligatory for women to cover their face and hands, does this agree with the saying it is advisable for men to lower their gaze? Or is that something separate? Is it something which needs to be discussed separately? Is it possible that it is not obligatory for women to cover, even though

---

[4] *Majma 'al-Bayan*, Quran 24:31.

this is definite in jurisprudence, but that it be advisable for men to lower their gaze?

We know from the life-style of the Holy Prophet (swas) that it is not obligatory for men to cover their head, hands, face or neck. Does this mean that it is also not advisable that men lower their gaze if they are walking down the street and women are passing? These are two different issues and must be discussed separately.

Another issue is that in areas other than the ones we mentioned as exceptions which the traditions have commented upon and in which the verse itself states what the limitations are, the face and the hands are among the absolute necessities of Islam whereby covering everything but them is obligatory for women. Of course, this itself has an exception which we will discuss in the next verse which is that if women reach beyond a certain age, it is no longer obligatory for them. But in general, covering the hair of a woman is among the compulsory precepts of Islam. It is clear that much of the hair which shows by which one would conclude that a woman's head is 'uncovered' is clearly not permissible to show in Islam. Covering the neck, the chest, the arms above the wrists, the feet (which is debated) from the ankles above are all among the obligatory aspects of Islam. There is no controversy here.

But there is another point. We said that we have to discuss separately whether or not lowering the gaze is advisable. If the look is of a flirting nature, looking with the anticipation of pleasure, this is another clear issue which is among those which are forbidden. Not only is it forbidden to look at strangers or persons to whom one is not *mahram*, but even those who are *mahram* as well. If a father was to flirt with his daughter, it is forbidden and perhaps an even greater sin. It is forbidden for a father-in-law to look at his son's wife

LESSON FOUR: THE ISLAMIC HIJAB – PART II

with lust. That is, in Islam, lust is exclusively allowed between marital partners. It is not permissible in any form anywhere else between anyone else.

But this should be distinguished from *riba'* which means to look but not with the intention of lust nor to really see or view the other person. It is a special state which could be dangerous. That is, the fear exists that the look will cause a person to deviate to a forbidden state. This, then, is also forbidden and there is no difference of opinion on this.

Thus, if a person says it is advisable to look, a lustful look is not meant or a look which holds the fear that it may lead to something forbidden.

Now we will discuss 'looking'. We have a tradition recorded by Ali ibn Ja'far, the brother of Imam Reza (as). He asks to what point a man can look at a woman who is not permissible to him? He said, "Her face and her hands and her feet."[5] Of course, face and hands are clearly so but the jurisprudents have not issued edicts about the feet.

There is another tradition about a man who is on a trip and dies. There is no man present to give him the obligatory bath for the dead nor are any *mahram* women present. What should be done for the obligatory ritual bath? The opposite has also been questioned, a woman on a trip who dies and there are no *mahram* men present to give her bath. When in both cases they asked Imam Sadiq (as), he said about the first case, "Those women may touch and wash that part of the man's body which was permissible for them to see when

---

[5] *Qurb al-Asnad*, p.102.

he was alive." The same thing is said about a woman who has died. The Imam (as) said that if they touch the face and wash her face and her hands, this is sufficient. It is not necessary to wash her whole body. Thus, a man may look at a woman's face and hands when she is alive.'[6]

We also find this in the tradition in *Mustamsak* which Ayatullah Hakim relates about Fatimah, peace be upon her. One is the tradition regarding the Companion Salman who once entered her house and saw that she was grinding barley and her hands were bleeding. This tradition makes it clear that the hands were not covered and that it was not forbidden to look at her hands because if it had been, neither would Salman have looked at them nor would she have left them uncovered.

More authentic than this is a tradition of Jabir that appears in *al-Kafi*, in *Wasa'il* and in all of the reliable books on traditions which the *'ulama* narrate. Jabir narrated that he went with the Prophet of God to enter the blessed Fatimah's house. The Holy Prophet (swas) had said that a person should seek permission to enter another's house, even if it belonged to one's mother and that the only exception is that one need not seek permission to enter one's wife's room. "When he arrived at her house, he did not enter but called out, *'Assalam alaykum ya ahl al-bayt'*. She answered from inside the house. The Holy Prophet (swas) asked, 'Do you allow us to enter?' She said, Yes enter.' He asked, 'Should the person with mc enter?' She said, 'No. Then wait until I cover my head.' Then she said, 'Enter.' Again the Holy Prophet (swas) asked 'Should the person with me enter?' And she said, 'Yes.' Jabir says that when he entered he saw that her face was sallow colored. 'I became very sad when I

---

[6] *Wasa'il al-Shiah*, vol.17, p.135.

realized it was because of lack of food. I said to myself, 'Look at how the caliph and a king's daughter is brought up and the daughter of Prophet of God!"[7]

This shows that the Prophet's daughter neither covered her face nor her hands. Otherwise Jabir's look would have been forbidden.

Among the traditions, we have a great many which, when they ask of the Imam (as), he says that one cannot look at the forearm of a woman or at a woman's hair. All of these are mentioned but nowhere does it say anything about the face and hands.

Another issue is *ihram* (the pilgrim's clothes) where it is forbidden for women to cover their face and therefore we realize that it is not obligatory. It could not be that there be something which is obligatory but not so in the ihram and forbidden here.

"**Let them cast their veils over their bosoms**." The verse itself expresses the limits and does not include the face and hands. On the other hand, those who say looking' is absolutely forbidden have given a reason, the very reason which has been given for it not being forbidden. They refer to the verse, "**say to the believing men to cast down their glance.**" He answers that in the first place, the verse does not say what not to look at. Secondly, it says min which mean 'from something', and thirdly, *ghadd* means 'cast down' or 'lower'.

There is another tradition which is referred to and those who say that it is forbidden to look should note it. A man wrote a letter to

---

[7] *Al-Kafi*, vol. 5 p. 528 and *Wasa'il al-Shiah*, vol. 3, p. 28.

Imam Hasan Askari (as) where he said that there is a woman who wants to confess something and others want to listen to her confession to bear witness to it. Must she confess behind a curtain and the others listen from behind a curtain to then justly say that it was her voice? The Imam (as) said, "No. She should come forward to bear witness but she should cover herself so that only the roundness of her face is visible."

Another tradition which they present is an often quoted tradition. It is called Sa'd Iskaf in reference to a man who went to the Prophet with his face bleeding and said that he had a complaint to make. The Holy Prophet (swas) told him to speak. He said he was walking down the street of Madinah and saw a woman coming towards him who was very beautiful and who had tied her scarf behind her head and her chest was visible. As she passed, he turned his head to look at her and did not see what was in front of him. Something was sticking out of the wall and it struck his face and injured him. The verse was then revealed, "*Say to the believing men to cast down their glance.*"[8]

Another reason they give is that it says in the traditions, "Is there anything which has not committed an illicit act for the illicit act of the eyes is to look?" The answer is that this is referring to looking with lust, not just looking; like the tradition which says, "looking is like an arrow of satan," and, of course, it refers to looking with lust.

---

[8] *Al-Kafi*, vol. 5, p. 521; *Wasail al-Shiah*, vol. 3, p. 24. It should be noted that most often this tradition which refers to a woman who tied her scarf around the back of her neck, allowing men with have a lust look towards her. In general, the situation presented in verse 24:31 also applies to present day modern dresses.

LESSON FOUR: THE ISLAMIC HIJAB – PART II

There is another tradition which I have read in the books on traditions of the Sunnis. It says the Holy Prophet (swas) was on a journey, probably the Farewell Pilgrimage. Ibn Abbas, a young boy then, was behind him. He continued to look at the women who passed back and forth in the ihram. The Holy Prophet (swas) realized that he was doing this and he turned the boy's face away. Ibn Abbas then began to look from that direction. The Holy Prophet (swas) again turned the boy's face away.

According to the Shi'ite sources, the tradition differs. It says that he was a very handsome young boy and the Holy Prophet (swas) was riding, probably on a camel. A woman from the Khasamiyyah tribe came to ask the Holy Prophet (swas) a question. She asked and the Holy Prophet (swas) answered. Then the Holy Prophet (swas) realized that her eyes were fixed upon Fazl ibn 'Abbas and Fazl ibn 'Abbas was staring at her. The tradition states that the Holy Prophet (swas) turned Fazl's face away saying, "A young woman and a young man, I am afraid satan will enter."[9]

They say that because of this, it is clear that it is forbidden to look like this. There is no doubt about it.

This is love making and it is forbidden. Shaykh Ansari says that from this tradition it is clear that it was obligatory for women to cover themselves and it was not forbidden in general for men to look. Otherwise, the Holy Prophet (swas) would not have looked but he was looking at her as he was answering her questions and saw that her eyes were fixed on Fazl ibn 'Abbas and his on hers.

---

[9] *Sahih Bukhari*, vol. 8, p.63.

Ayatullah Hakim narrates another tradition. A man by the name of Ali ibn Salah said to Imam Reza (as), "I have a problem. I look at beautiful women and it makes me happy to do so but I have no bad intentions." The Imam (as) said, "There is no problem as God is aware of your intentions and you have no ill intentions but fear an illicit act."

LESSON FIVE

THE ISLAMIC HIJAB - PART III

We have said that there are two issues involved here. First, what is obligatory upon women and what is permissible for men. Those points which are clear are that it is obligatory upon women to cover themselves except for their face and hands. This is neither compulsory nor in the Holy Qur'an; nor in the traditions can we find reason to believe that it is obligatory upon women to cover their face and hands.

But as to whether it is permitted for men to look, it is clear and definite that if the look is a lustful one, that is, a look with intention of lust, there is no doubt that this is forbidden. If a look is not a lustful one but the surrounding conditions and situation are such that a fear exist that one may be led to deviate, that too is forbidden. These two are both forbidden, not only towards women to whom men are not *mahram* but to women they are *mahram* with, as well, other than their wife. It is even forbidden for a man to look in this way at another man.

Thus there are only these two questions. Is it obligatory upon a woman to cover her face and hands and secondly, is it permissible or not for a man to look without lust or fear of deviation?

LESSON FIVE: THE ISLAMIC HIJAB – PART III

FROM THE VIEW POINT OF TRADITIONS

From the point of view of the traditions, and the external aspects of the verse, it is more or less certain that it is not necessary for women to cover the face and hands and it is not forbidden for men to look at a woman's face or hands if his look is not one of lust or fear of deviation.

The traditions are numerous and we have only referred to a few and a few more will be mentioned. One is a tradition from Imam Reza (as), who is asked, "Is it permissible for a man to look at the hair of his wife's sister?" "No. It is not permissible unless she be a woman who is past child-bearing age. A wife's sister is just like any other woman that you are not related to according to the Divine Law and you can only look at her and her hair if she is beyond child-bearing age."[1]

Thus whenever the Imams are asked if it is permissible to look at a woman's hair, etc., they are never asked if it is permissible to look at a woman's face when the look is not one of lust or fear of deviation.

There is another tradition from Imam Reza (as), about a young boy. "Must a seven year old boy be encouraged to recite the ritual prayer?" He said it is not obligatory but to encourage is a good thing. It is not necessary that a woman hide her hair from him until he reaches puberty.[2] We see that again it is covering the hair which is referred to and not covering the face.

---

[1] *Wasail al-Shiah,* vol. 3, p. 25.
[2] *Wasail al-Shiah,* vol. 3, p. 29.

ON THE ISLAMIC HIJAB

CONCERNING 'WHAT THEIR RIGHT HANDS OWN'

Again concerning "What their right hands own," if a female slave is *mahram* to a man, is a male slave *mahram* to his female owner or not? I am using the term '*mahram*' here erroneously with a purpose because this is an interpretation that others have. There is a difference when we say '*mahram*' meaning, for instance, they are not permitted to marry. It is permitted for him to look at her hair but he is not *mahram* in the usual sense such as the father-in-law and his son's wife. Some have interpreted it this way. When a question is asked about this, the answer given is that there is no problem if a male slave looks at his female owner's hair. Again, hair is mentioned, not the face.

There is a discussion concerning a *khwajah* (eunuch) and whether or not he is a male slave or a woman.

The ruling was that he was like a woman and there was no problem if he looked at a woman's hair. A person asked Imam Reza (as) if is was necessary to cover before a *khwajah* and the Imam (as) said it was not. "They used to enter my father's house and women did not cover their hair before them."[3]

As to "the women of the Book," of course, they do not need to be *dhimmah*. There is no problem with looking at the hair of a Jewish woman or a Christian or a Zoroastrian woman or a woman who is none of these. The Holy Prophet (swas) said, "It is not forbidden to look at the hands and hair of *dhimmah* women."[4]

---

[3] *Wasail al-Shiah*, vol. 3, p. 29.
[4] *Wasail al-Shiah*, vol. 3, p. 29.

LESSON FIVE: THE ISLAMIC HIJAB – PART III

Wherever you look you see that the issue which is an exception is referred to or questioned and the face and hands are not questioned. Whereas, if it had been forbidden to look at the face and hands of a woman, they would have been referred to in the exceptions.

As to *dhimmah* women, some of the *'ulama* believe that we must look and see what the situation was at the time of the Holy Prophet (swas); what extent of the body was not covered? Clearly the *dhimmah* women did not cover their hair or their hands to a certain point. There was no problem, then, in looking at them.

I have mentioned that in every exception, it is permitted to look without lust except under one condition. That is, it is permissible to look at a woman in lust when one wants to see a woman to decide whether or not to marry her, as a serious suitor for marriage.[5] Of course, it is clear that a man cannot spend years looking at women in this way to determine whether or not he wants to get married. There are other conditions as well. How much education should she have? Where does she come from, etc. After all of the other conditions are met and the only one remaining is to see if one wants to marry her, it is this situation that the exception refers to. If the purpose is only lust, it is clearly not with the intention of marrying.

These, then, were some of the traditions but there are many more from both Sunni and Shi'ite sources.

---

[5] There is clearly a difference between laws made by people or a law-making body and God's Laws. If a person wants to follow the laws of a country, one can play a bit with them. "The law is such and such and I did not do that." But when it comes to God's Law there is a difference and one's intention is known.

The traditions say it refers to Muslim woman and not the *dhimmah* but not with lust or with a look which holds the fear of deviating within in. It is permissible to look at her in what she customarily wears outside of her home. Ayatullah Burujerdi says that one must suffice to look only at that which was common in those days. Perhaps customs have changed today and even more areas of their body are uncovered.

There is another point to mention following this. There is an edict, based on a tradition which some *'ulama* find difficult to accept. It is concerned with a tradition where the Imam said that there is no problem to look at the hair of a bedouin woman, a woman from suburb of Kufah or Ilj (non-Arab bedouin women). Why? Because it is their custom to dress in their particular style and they refuse to cover their heads. So it is not forbidden to look at them, but, of course, not with lust.

Some of the *'ulama* have issued edicts just as the tradition states but the late Ayatullah Mohammad Kazim does not issue one because he says what is perhaps meant is that in places where these kinds of women are, it is not obligatory for men to curtail their comings and goings. There is no problem if their eyes fall on these women's hair. There is no problem if the women are told to cover themselves and they do not listen. Therefore, he felt it was an exceptional situation, not one that needed a religious edict.

Another religious jurisprudent says the same thing holds for urban women. If they are told they should cover themselves and they do not, there is no problem if men look at their hair.

LESSON FIVE: THE ISLAMIC HIJAB – PART III

HEARING THE VOICE OF A NON-MAHRAM WOMAN

Another issue is that of hearing the voice of a non-*mahram* woman. Is this forbidden or not? This is clear from the edicts that it is not forbidden as long as it is not for lust or in fear of deviating. There is no problem between a blind person who is hearing another. However, there is, caution. Where it does not concern a man, he should avoid it. But it is forbidden for a woman to make her voice very pleasant and attractive so as to cause confusion in a man whereby a man who has a sickness in his heart hears her voice, and gets attracted to it through lust.[6]

This is among the things which are very clear. It is permissible to hear the voice of a non-*mahram* woman as long as her voice is normal and not one to cause lust or arouse the fear of deviating.

The verse of the Holy Qur'an is clear. It does not say women should not speak. No. It says they should not change the tone of their voice. Women continuously went to the Holy Prophet (swas) and to the Imams and asked the questions they had. This is clear.

SHAKING HANDS

Another issue is shaking hands. Of course, all of these issues arise only when there is no lust or fear of deviation present; otherwise they are clearly not permitted. Again, the traditions and religious edicts confirm one another in this matter. The Imam was asked if it is permitted to shake hands with a nonrelated woman. He said, "No, unless the hands be covered or the woman be *mahram*." One must not shake the hands with a woman who is not *mahram*

---

[6] Ayatullah Sayyid Muhammad Kazim Tabatabaie Yazdi, *Urwatul Wusqa*, Section on Marriage, Chapter One, Issue 39.

unless her hand is covered and even then, pressure should not be applied.'[7]

THESE ARE ISSUES OF RELIGIOUS EDICTS

Here there are two more points which should be mentioned. The first is that the issues mentioned up to this point were all referred to within the contents of the verses and the traditions. Perhaps no further questions would occur to a person up to this point, but these are some of the issues which have occurred to me. Since this is a matter of an edict, everyone must note that I have mentioned my own point of view and referred to these proofs because of their necessity but the issue is one which must be followed according to the Divine Law. The second point is that edicts exist which are comparable to the ones mentioned that include the religious edicts of the great *'ulama* but these are the edicts of the minority, not the majority.

For instance, Shaykh Tusi gave such an edict as well as Shaykh Hedayat and Shaykh Ansari. All three are among the most learned Shi'ite scholars. The others mention these reasons like Ayatullah Hakim in *Mustamsak* but when it comes to issuing a religious edict they hold back. The actions of Muslims, to this point, have been opposed to these views so the religious jurisprudent moves beyond the issue.

MUSLIM CUSTOM

This itself is an issue that the customs and habits of Muslims oppose something which is clear from the verses of Qur'an and the

---

[7] *Ibid.*

LESSON FIVE: THE ISLAMIC HIJAB – PART III

traditions. The customs of the Muslims are not something which can be easily put aside. There is a need for an analysis as to what it is.

If we assume that Muslims have acquired a custom from the beginning of Islam whereby it is discovered to be from the customs of the Holy Prophet (swas) and the Imams, it should be preserved. However, a custom of the people is not proof in itself except when it is discovered to be among the customs of the Holy Prophet. Then it becomes proof and must be observed.

For instance, take the beard. Some people say that the real proof for it is that men from the time of the Holy Prophet (swas) and later all had beards. Thus, we rely upon this.

Now note what they answer. If someone had said that it is forbidden to grow a beard we would have said that people in the past, according to custom, have a beard and this existed from the time of the Holy Prophet. Thus, it was not forbidden to have a beard. If it had been forbidden, it could not have become the custom. But the question then arises whether growing a beard is obligatory or recommended. We assume the possibility that it is a part of custom which is, at least, recommended or unspecified. Custom only dictates when there is a lack of respect involved. Therefore, it is either obligatory or recommended.

A thought has occurred to me here which is a historical social point and most often the reason why the religious authorities become fixed here is because they do not attend to the social issue. The modest dress did not exist among the pre-Islamic Arabs. Islam brought the covering of the head, neck, and chest, etc. and the forbidding of looking with lust. But a part of that which Islam brought existed in non-Arab areas. It was a very strong influence in

Iran, in particular, among the Jews and people were influenced by their way of thinking.

Islam did not make it obligatory to uncover the face. It said it is obligatory to cover the hair, not to display the face. Clearly, those nations which came to accept Islam were following their own customs because Islamic precepts did not say it was obligatory to display the face, except in the *harem*. Nor did they say it was forbidden to cover the face. It gave a choice. It left it up to the various nations to practice their own customs of the modest dress if they so desired.

History shows that non-Arabs felt it was obligatory to cover the face. Thus, this custom of covering the face, as we find it now, is not a custom of the Holy Prophet (swas) and the Imams (as).

Another point which is very sensitive and should also be considered, relates to caution. Every religious jurisprudent speaks this way out of caution. They all know that these two things exist, one in a woman and one in a man. That which exists within a woman is the desire to show herself off, it is a part of her nature. That which exists within man is an inclination towards looking, not just looking but flirting and receiving pleasure from it.

Both of these exist. Will Durant says that there is nothing in the world more firm and more persevering that a man's desire to look at a woman. It exists no matter how much it is restrained and it is referred to in the traditions. It is because of this that a religious jurisprudent does not find the courage, in spite of the fact that all of these reasons and proofs exist, to issue a religious edict. They say caution should not be put aside. The caution relates to human nature itself.

LESSON FIVE: THE ISLAMIC HIJAB – PART III

This brings up another issue. Some people follow a philosophy and that philosophy is that in those areas which are ruled by customs, whatever one does not say to the people is better. It is better not to say it than to say it.

I may have mentioned that I once received a letter in praise of the book I wrote called Stories of Good People. The ritual prayer leader in Khuzistan read the book. He said that he looked up all of the stories. Although not one idea was changed and they had been presented in a very readable, pleasant style, he had two criticisms. The first criticism related to a story about the blessed Fatimah and Ali, peace be upon them.

Their work had been divided so that Imam Ali (as) did the work outside of the house and she, the work within the house, a division which the Holy Prophet (swas) had made at the very beginning of their marriage. When Imam Ali (as) was home, he helped her within the house and when he was not at home, she did the work outside the house as well.

One day she was covered from head to toe in soot from having started the fire and because there was no flowing water in Madinah, it had to be carried from the wells, often at some distance away, the pressure applied by the straps of her water bag remained on her body because of all the water she had carried to her house. This man said that even though this story was true and was part of the traditions, I should not have mentioned it because it could be misused.

I do not deny the general principle that if telling the truth will cause the people to deviate; it should not be said because the reason for telling the truth, in the first place, is to guide the people, not to turn others away from it. Of course, the Holy Qur'an tells us,

> "*Those who conceal the clear (Signs) that we have sent down and the Guidance after We have shown them clearly in the Book ... on them shall be God's curse and the curse of those entitled to curse ...*"(2:159)

The tone of this verse is very strong. There are very few verses in the Holy Qur'an where such a strong and angry tone is found. At the same time, I believe the purpose to be that people should not conceal the truth because of their own interests but to conceal the truth because of the truth itself under very limited, temporary and definite conditions so that it is not misused and does not fall under this verse. In other words, it is forbidden to lie but it is not always obligatory to speak the truth. That is, there are occasions when one must remain silent.

I am of the belief that this kind of prudence, when it is based upon the real issue of the truth, has no problem but, when it is based on individual, personal or group interests, it is a different story. Now the point is whether or not it is prudent thinking not to issue a religious edict about buying or selling a radio or that it is not obligatory for a woman to cover her face and hands. Is it a correct kind of thinking? Is it intelligible? Does it produce the correct result or not? Will some women who cover their face and hands then uncover their face and hands and finally their whole form by saying this truth? Or is the opposite true?

That is, many men and women think that the basis of the religious viewpoint is that the face of a woman should not show for when the face shows, there will be no stopping the rest. On the other

LESSON FIVE: THE ISLAMIC HIJAB – PART III

hand, the covering of the face is impractical and, from the point of view of logic, it is indefensible. No reasoning or deduction can be given for it being so. Therefore, they will then completely uncover themselves.

Some sociologists believe that the cause for the extremity in women's dress and their lack of modesty is because of the erroneous belief that society had about the modest dress. Yet the error was that the truth was not spoken! If it had been expressed just as the Islamic precepts express it, things would never have reached this point. It is here that one should refer to the proverb, "being, more Catholic than the Pope," or "jumping from the frying pan into the fire."

The Holy Qur'an says in *Surah Hujarat*,

"O believers, advance not beyond God and His Messenger" (49:1).

What is meant by 'advance' is a point beyond which God and His Prophet said one needed to go, thereby, 'advancing beyond God and His Messenger'.

Imam Ali (as) said, "God has given limits. Do not aggress beyond them. That is, he has specified the forbidden, do not disobey. He has specified the obligatory and the precepts; do not shun them and as to the things for which He remained silent about neither forbidden nor obligatory it was not because He forgot them but rather He wanted you to be free in regard to them. Therefore, do not restrict yourself there and make something your duty in the name of God's religion and God."

The Holy Prophet (swas) said in a tradition recorded in Jama'al-Saghir, "Just as God dislikes that which He prohibited, people should obey and He likes them to do what is allowed; whatever is without any problem should be considered to be such and they should not forbid anything which God has not forbidden..."

This tradition has also been recorded as the following, "God loves people who allow whatever He has allowed and prohibit whatever He has prohibited."

Perhaps I am mistaken. As I have mentioned, in areas covered by religious edicts, each person must follow the edicts of their own mujtahid.

But, in regard to that which is mentioned as prudent thinking and saying it is not advisable to mention something even though it is the truth, I disagree with this prudent thinking. I believe it is advisable to express the truth and that which is advisable is to counteract the concept that women today express, "The modest dress is impractical." We must prove to them that the Islamic modest dress is logical and practical.

Secondly, we must make efforts to establish cultural, social, and health activities, particular to women, and resist the mixed activities which are imitated from Europe. It is only in this way that women will rediscover their real personality and the possibility that they will no longer be a tool, a toy and a means to men's lust in the name of freedom and equality.

THE RELIGIOUS EDICTS ON THESE ISSUES

We have seen through these lessons that according to the precise and moderate precepts of Islam, in regard to the relations of

LESSON FIVE: THE ISLAMIC HIJAB – PART III

a man and a woman based upon the reliable sources and practices of the Holy Prophet and pure Imams, it is documented that it is not obligatory to cover the face and hands as well as the fact that they strengthen the permissibility for men or women to look at each other upon the condition that it is not for lust (unless they are husband and wife) nor fear of deviation. Now we will briefly refer to the edicts of the religious jurisprudents because it is important to know how they have interpreted this issue from the beginning of Islam to the present.[8]

To begin with, what is the opinion of religious jurisprudents as to the covering of the face and hands and secondly, what edicts have they issued in regard to looking?

As to the fact that it is not obligatory to cover the face and hands, there appears to be no difference of opinion among all of the religious jurisprudents, Shi'ite or Sunni. There was only one Sunni who disagreed. He was Abu Bakr ibn 'Abd al-Rahman ibn Hisham and it is not clear if his opinion related solely to the ritual prayer or if it included those people who were not *mahram*, as well.

There is no difference of opinion as to the face but some differences have appeared with regard to the hands to the wrist and the feet to the ankles as to whether or not they are included among the exceptions. Before mentioning what they have said, two points should be noted. First, the issue of covering is dealt with in two places in jurisprudence.

---

[8] The last section of this lesson was added later by Martyr Murtaza Mutahhari and is not on the tapes but because of the importance of the issues referred to, it has been translated and appears here.

ON THE ISLAMIC HIJAB

One is in relation to the fact that it is obligatory in the ritual prayer for women to cover all of their body, whether or not a non-*mahram* is present. Here the question arises whether or not the face and hands must also be covered. The second place the issue is discussed is in relation to marriage and to what extent a suitor has the right to look at the woman he may decide to seek permission to marry. Here, there is most often a general discussion about covering and the permissibility or impermissibility of looking.

Thus, from the point of view of jurisprudence, we have two kinds of covering. One is the covering which is obligatory for the ritual prayer which has certain rules such as the clothes worn must be ritually pure, not usurped, etc. The other is the covering which is obligatory, other than for the ritual prayer, before men with whom a woman is not *mahram* and which does not have the special requirements of the covering for the ritual prayer. As we will later point out, there appears to be no difference as far as extent of covering before a *mahram*.

The second point to be noted is that the religious jurisprudents employ a term which refers to the body other than the face and two hands. This term is *'aurah'*, 'exposed' or 'bare' or 'naked'. It is possible that this term appears unattractive to some people in the sense that nakedness may be considered to be unattractive. We then ask if a woman's body, other than her face and hands, be something which is considered to be ugly or unattractive from the point of view of Islamic jurisprudence?

The answer is that the word *aurah* in no way refers to something ugly or unattractive. In the first place, not every ugly or undesirable act is referred to as *aurah* and the opposite is also true.

LESSON FIVE: THE ISLAMIC HIJAB – PART III

The word *aurah* is often used in reference to something which has nothing to do with ugliness.

In the Holy Qur'an, the word is used in verse 33:13, "**Truly our houses are open** "(exposed, vulnerable, *aurah*), by which excuse they hoped to be exempt from fighting. It is clear that no ugliness is referred to in relation to their houses. In verse 24:59, which will be referred to, three times are mentioned where even a *mahram* needs to seek permission to enter an area of another's privacy (except a husband or wife) and these are called the time of "three *aurah*".

In the *Majma' al-Bayan* the author, who is incomparable among the commentators in his ability to cleave apart the meanings of words in reference to the use of the word *aurah* in verse 33:13 says, "*aurah* refers to anything which can easily be harmed which one is concerned about like the borders or frontiers of a country or something related to a war. A bare or exposed or naked place or house is a house which is vulnerable and easily harmed."[9]

Thus, it becomes clear that the word is not used by the religious jurisprudents to abase or weaken. The body of a woman is referred to as vulnerable[10] because it is like a house which contains no walls and can be easily harmed and must be covered by some kind of an enclosure.

---

[9] *Majma'al-Bayan*, Commentary of the Holy Qur'an, 33:13.

[10] The fact that Islam regards body of women as vulnerable and must be protected by a covering is very logical and realistic considering the data on sexual crimes against women in Western and liberal societies where hijab is not practiced and not legally implanted.

Now let us look at what the edicts say. Allamah in *Tazkirat ul fuqaha'* wrote, "The totality of woman's body is *aurah* (vulnerable) other than her face." All of the *'ulama* in the various cities confirm this other than Abu Bakr ibn Abd al-Rahman Hisham who believes all of the body of a woman is vulnerable. His opinion is in the minority.

In the opinion of Shi'ite *'ulama*, the two hands up to the wrist are like the face and are not considered vulnerable (*aurah*). Malik ibn Anis Shafe'i, Uwaz'i and Sugyan Thawri agree with the Shi'ite *'ulama* because ibn Abbas had recorded from the Holy Prophet (swas) who said, "The face and two hands are included in the exception." But, according to the view of Ahmad Hanbal and Dawoud Zahiri, the two hands must be covered. The words recorded by ibn 'Abbas are sufficient to disregard this opinion.

Allamah refers to the two feet saying, "As can be seen, the religious jurisprudents refer to *Surah Nur* for the covering required for the ritual prayer yet it does not refer to the ritual prayer. That which must be covered in the ritual prayer is that which must be covered before a non-*mahram* and if there is a difference of opinion, it is about whether or not more areas need to be covered for the ritual prayer. But, as to the fact that which is not obligatory to cover in the ritual prayers is the same as that which is not obligatory to cover with a non-*mahram*, there is no difference of opinion."[11]

Ibn Rushd, the famous Andulusian religious jurisprudent, physician and philosopher wrote, "It is the opinion of the majority of *'ulama* that the body of a woman, other than her face and two hands, is vulnerable, *aurah*. Ahmad Hanifah believes that the two feet are

---

[11] *Bidayat al Mujtahid*, vol.1, p.111.

LESSON FIVE: THE ISLAMIC HIJAB – PART III

also not included. Abu Bakr Abd al-Rahman Hisham believes that the total body of woman is *aurah* without any exceptions.

Shaykh Jawad Mughniyah wrote in his book *al-Fiqh ala Mazahib al-Khamsah*, "All of the Islamic *'ulama* agree that it is obligatory for men and women to cover that part of the body for the ritual prayer which they cover outside of the ritual prayer. The difference arises as to how much needs to be covered. The question in regard to women is whether or not it is obligatory for her to cover her face and hands to the extent necessary for the ritual prayer and the question in regard to men is if it is obligatory for them to cover more than the navel to the knee." Then he says, "According to Imamiyah Shi'ite *'ulama*, it is obligatory for women to cover that much in the ritual prayers which she covers before non-*mahram* other than during the ritual prayer."

What is strange is that some contemporary *'ulama* have thought that the view of the *'ulama* in the past was that it was obligatory to cover the face and this is wrong.

As to the permissibility of looking, Allamah wrote, "A man looking at a woman or a woman looking at a man is either necessary (like the look of a suitor) or not. If there is no necessity, it is not permissible to look at more than the face and hands and if there is fear of deviating, this much is also not permissible. If there is no fear of deviating, according to Shaykh Tusi, there is nothing to prevent it but it is disapproved. The majority of the Shafe'i believe the same but some believe that it is forbidden to look at the face and hands."

In regard to looking at the face and hands, there are basically three opinions. First, the opinion that it is absolutely forbidden according to Allamah and a few other people including the author of the *Jawahir*. Second, it is permissible to look once and what is forbidden is repeated looking. Muhaqiq in *Sharae'*, Shahid Awwal in *Lum'ah* and Allamah in his other books hold this view. Third, it is absolutely permissible according to Shaykh Tusi, Kulayni, the author of *Hada'iq*, Shaykh Ansari, Naraqi in *Mustamad* and Shahid Thani in *Masalik*. Shahid Thani dismisses the reasoning of the Shafe'i which Allamah had accepted but he says at the end, "There is no doubt that caution should prevail."

The above were the views of the past jurisprudents. Most contemporary jurisprudents do not refer directly to these two issues and, most often, cover it over by means of 'caution'. But among the contemporary jurisprudents, Ayatullah Hakim in his recital *Minhaj al-Salihin*,[12] in the section on marriage, gives a direct edict in which he states the face and hands are an exception. "It is permissible to look at a person one intends to marry as well as *dhimmah* women as long as there is no lust in the glance including women whom one cannot prevent from not covering and women who are non-*mahram*. It is forbidden to look at any other woman, other than their face and two hands to the wrist, and that only if there is no lust involved."

---

[12] *Minhaj al-Salahin*, 9th edition, issue 3.

LESSON SIX

THE ISLAMIC HIJAB - PART IV

ALLOWABLE EXPEDIENCES AND NON-EXPEDIENCES

As a conclusion to our previous discussion, there are two points to be mentioned. One is that the science of the principles of religious jurisprudence has two expressions which are of use to us here. Some things do not have the advisability to make them obligatory nor do they have the maliciousness to be ruled as forbidden. As they do not contain the criteria to oblige or forbid, they are allowable and because of this they are called allowable non-expediences (*mubah la-iqtidati*). Perhaps most of the allowed are of this type.

But there are others. The reason for their being allowable is because of certain wisdom which releases them. That is, if the Divine Law did not allow them, a necessary malice would have appeared. These kinds of allowed are known as allowed expediences. It is possible that with these allowed, an advisability or a maliciousness exists in activating or shunning these deeds but in order to obey a higher advisability which permitting then brings about, the Divine Law rules it as allowed and overlooks the other criteria.

Those allowed, which have been allowed because of not wanting to have fault or blame (*haraj*), are like this: Religious

LESSON SIX: THE ISLAMIC HIJAB – PART IV

jurisprudents consider the fact that if they want to forbid some deeds, the life of people will become very difficult so they do not forbid them.

Perhaps the best example is divorce. The Holy Prophet (swas) said, "Among all of the permissibles, divorce is the most detested." Someone may ask, "If it is detested then why is it permissible? Divorce should be forbidden." But no. At the same time that it is a detested act and the issuing of a divorce causes the heavens to shake, it is not forbidden. When Abu Ayyub Ansari wanted to divorce his wife, the Holy Prophet (swas) said "Divorcing Umm Ayyub is a sin." But, if Abu Ayyub had divorced his wife, the Holy Prophet (swas) would not have said it was invalid. That is something which is not forbidden at the same time it contains as many aspects as a forbidden thing contains and perhaps more. Because of this, it is detested but not forbidden.

The reason is that Islam does not want marriage to be compulsory. That is, to oblige a man, who must be the support and protector of a woman, to keep his wife at all costs. Efforts are made towards a divorce not occurring but that a man should keep his wife because he is so inclined and not grow cold towards his wife. But the situation goes beyond this and a man wants to divorce his wife. It is a hated deed so that one is only obliged to do it. This is one example of allowable expedience.

These exceptions exist in the area of the modest dress, as well. In relation to the extent of the modest dress, like the fact that it is not obligatory for a woman to cover her face, it is not forbidden for a man to look at a woman's face as long as it is not a look of lust. The difference between leaving the face uncovered or covered is one of the allowable expediences. That is, the very criterion that exists in relation to hair, exists in relation to the face. The criteria which exists in relation to the rest of the body, exists in relation to the face. There are many parts of the body which, even if they are not more stimulating, they are not less so than the face, but at the same time, this exception has appeared. The criteria is the same but if a woman is told to cover her hair, it is not difficult for her to do unless it is a woman whose rebellious nature and ego insists that her hair must remain uncovered.

It is a duty which does not cause difficulty. It does not in any way interfere with her life. But if a woman is told that she must cover her face as well, this prevents her from doing many things. It prevents her freedom of action.

For instance, many of the work available in society depends upon this very religious edict as to whether or not it is obligatory that a woman cover her face. Is it permissible for women to drive a car or not? The question has to be approached from the point of view of duties that a woman has whether or not it is permissible. Can she maintain her duties and drive, or not? If it is obligatory for women to cover their face and hands, is it not possible for them to drive a car? That is since driving would cause the nonperformance of a duty, she must not do so.

But another says, "No. It is not obligatory for women to cover her face." This then means that she can drive and driving does not mean that other parts of her body be visible or that she wears makeup or that her hair be uncovered. Just as long as the roundness of her face is visible, she can drive.

For instance, is it permissible for a woman to be a teacher and teach male students? After we said that hearing the voice of a non-

LESSON SIX: THE ISLAMIC HIJAB – PART IV

mahram woman is not a problem and that it is permissible for a man to look at the face of a non-*mahram* woman as long as it is not a lustful look, then she may be a teacher of male students. That is, the limits are this very face and hands. The truth is that the real question is whether or not women have to be limited to the home or not. This is not a small issue.

If we deduce that the view of Islam is that the face and hands of women must be covered along with the rest of her body, which is obligatory to be covered and if we say that a woman must be covered from head to toe, this means that the activities of a woman must be limited to her home because it is not possible for her to be active outside of her home. But if we say, no, it is not obligatory for women to cover their face and hands, we have not limited her activities with this. For instance, women who believe that they are obliged to cover themselves completely cannot ever leave their homes to go shopping for vegetables. She has to send a male servant or her husband to do this. Thus there is a great difference in whether or not it is obligatory for a woman to cover her face and hands. The area of her activities could become extremely limited.

We have deduced from the verses of the Holy Qur'an and the traditions. The only thing we found a lack of was religious edicts and this was not in relation to it being compulsory to cover the face and hand. Most edicts agree that it is not.

The area in which there is a lack of religious edicts sensed is in the area of whether or not it is permissible for a man to look at the face of an un-related women as long as his look is not of lust. The majority says it is not permissible but there are people like the great Alim Shaykh Ansari who say it is permissible and in the verse itself and in the traditions, it was very clearly permissible. Thus if we are asked, "What is the difference between the face and the hair? Does not the criterion which exists for the hair exist for the face? For the eyes and eyebrows? These criteria even carry more weight here." The answers are that it is an allowable expedience, not an allowable non-expedience, that a criterion which exists for one does not exist for another.

Also, in the exception which exists in relation to individuals, there are two exceptions which we will discuss later. Covering from one's father, one's children, the sons of one's husband, brothers, father-in-law, etc. is not obligatory. Here two criteria exist. First the look of a father and even an uncle differs from that of a non-*mahram*. It is natural that a father does not look at his daughter with lust or with the fear of deviating nor a son at his mother. Among brothers and uncles the same is true.

But there are some relationships which cannot be said to be this way. For instance, the son of a husband. Can the son of a husband naturally have the same feelings that a father has for his daughter? Even if his daughter is among the most beautiful women of the world? If a man takes a young wife who is of the same age as his son, will it be this way? Clearly not. Perhaps it can be said that a father-in-law is the same way. Here again the reason why it is not necessary to cover before these relations is because of difficulty. A man marries and his son lives in the same house, where the son is a part and parcel of the home. The wife wants to become a part of the home. If they are to live within one place and the wife has to cover, it will cause great difficulties. This is one point.

From here we can draw a conclusion which is just as we said in relation to divorce. Divorce is permissible but it is detested. It is not forbidden but it is detested. So that if a man were to ask, "If I want to divorce my wife, will I have earned God's satisfaction? Should I divorce her or not?" It is best not to divorce her. In this same area, looking at a non-*mahram* woman when it does not stem from lust or arouse a fear of deviating, is permissible. But, if someone were to ask, "Is it better to look or not to look?" It is, of course, better not to look. The Divine Law allowed it so people would not be put to undue difficulties but the criteria still exist. Is it better for a woman to cover her face or not? It is better to cover her face but because covering her face causes her great difficulties, it has been allowed to be uncovered. The same is true of looking at the face of a non-*mahram* woman which, at the same time though permissible, not doing is better.

TRADITIONS AND NARRATIONS

There are a series of traditions in this area which completely explain this issue. In the previous lesson we presented the traditions that basically stated it was forbidden for a man to look at the face of a non-*mahram* woman. There are another series of traditions whose transmissions are questionable and are not relied upon by the *'ulama* but they do explain things and offer good ethics.

There is the famous letter of Imam Ali (as) to Imam Hasan (as) which is a letter of advice, "To the extent possible keep your wife or wives away from mixing with others. Nothing protects a woman better than the home." The tradition contains the word *ihtijab*. It means to be hidden by a curtain. He said to Malik Ashtar, "Do not continue to separate (*ihtijab*) yourself from the people."

Where the Imam says to avoid women having to mix with non-*mahram*' men, this is more healthy for women. This is truth. However much she is separated from non-*mahram* men, the danger of deviation lessens, whereas today we see how the danger has increased with their system in the modern world. Therefore, we cannot say that mixing of men and women together creates less chances of danger.

There is another tradition which is reliable. Religious jurisprudents rely upon it.[1] The Holy Prophet (swas) said, "The first look is yours but the second is to your loss." Is this giving a ruling or taking a position? Some have said this is giving a ruling. They say the Holy Prophet (swas) said that one may look once at a woman but a second look is forbidden. Others say what is meant is that the first time when your eyes unintentionally fall on a woman's face it is possible, but a second time when it is done intentionally is not permitted. But still others say that it is neither a ruling nor taking a position. The first time is unintentional but the second time it is with lust and this is why the Holy Prophet (swas) said the second time is to your loss.

There is another tradition which is a good lesson although it is not relied upon in jurisprudence. It is good ethics. It says the Holy Prophet (swas) asked, "What things are better than any other for women?" No one answered. Imam Hasan (as), still a child, went home and asked what the answer was. Fatimah, peace be upon her, said, "That she sees no man and no man sees her."[2] This shows that for a woman looking at a man is also dangerous. It is safer and better if she does not meet non-*mahram* men. There is no question that this is so. What we are referring to is what is allowed so that a

---

[1] *Wasa'il al-Shiah*, vol. 3, p. 24.
[2] *Wasa'il al-Shiah*, vol. 3, p. 9.

woman will face less difficulty and not what is safer and more secure. Clearly this is safer.³

There is another tradition, "A look is an arrow of satan."⁴ This, of course, refers to a look of lust. Or, "Everything has its adulterous form and the adultery of the eyes is to look,"⁵ referring to a look of lust and one which holds the fear of deviating.

THE EXCEPTION OF A SUITOR

In the traditions we have many which relate to the time when one is a suitor for marriage at which time it is permitted to look. Does this not mean, then, that it is not permitted if one is not a suitor? Not only is it permitted but it has been stressed that it is better if one looks. For instance, they said a man wanted to marry a daughter of one of the Companions who was a resident of Madinah. The Holy Prophet (swas) said to him, "Go and look and then marry. There is something in the eyes of the Companions."⁶ The Holy Prophet (swas) told him to look first because the Companions were from just one or two tribes and most of them had some kind of an eye defect. He told him to look first and then marry so that later he would not be disappointed.

---

³ It is possible that someone presents an intellectual reason that nullifies this deduction by saying, for instance, what difference is there between the hair and face that one is obligatory to cover one and not the other. Thus, we reason by practice and someone else presents an intellectual reason. It is sufficient for the person who is referring to practice, even if it be through presenting a possibility, that they invalidate it. There is a difference. If it were practical, Islam would have clarified it, but it did not want people to fall into difficulty.

⁴ *Wasa'il al-Shiah*, vol. 3, p. 24.

⁵ *Al-Kafi*, vol. 5, p. 539 and *Wasa'il al-Shiah*, vol. 3, p. 24.

⁶ *Sahih Muslim*, vol. 4, p.142.

Mugharyar ibn Shu'bay said, "I had sought to marry. The Holy Prophet (swas) said to me, 'Have you seen her?' I said, 'No. I have not.' He said, 'Go and see her because it will give strength to your marriage.⁷

Imam Ja'far Sadiq (as) said, "If one of you sought a woman for marriage, it is better if you see that woman, if your look is one of a suitor."⁸

When a tradition says that it is permissible as a suitor, then does this mean it is not permitted when one is not a suitor? If 100 king' as a suitor means that only the face and hands can be seen and nothing more, then it is limited to its not being lustful in anyway. This would mean that looking at other times is not permitted but this is not the way it is. It is permitted for a suitor to look at the face and hair of a woman and even the outline of her form, things that effect the form of a woman's body. It is more extensive and it is clear that which is permitted for a man who is a suitor is not permitted at other times. They have also said that if a suitor be a serious one, even if he looks with lust, there is no problem.

OTHER EXCEPTIONS REFERRED TO IN THE HOLY QUR'AN

Now we will discuss the other exceptions. Some relate to the extent of the modest dress. There is another exception which relates to the number of individuals. Some have no debate and others require a bit of explanation. The phrase, *"reveal not their adornment,"* appears twice and both times it is accompanied by an exception. The first time it relates to the extent of the modest dress

---

⁷ *Jama'h Tirmizi*, p. 175.
⁸ *Al-Wafi*, vol.12, p. 58; *Wasa'il al-Shia*, vol. 3, p.11; *Al-Kafi*, vol. 5, p. 365.

LESSON SIX: THE ISLAMIC HIJAB – PART IV

and that which is not necessary to cover. The second relates to people before whom it is not necessary to cover, including those that are not exceptions, such as hair, neck, chest, etc.

It first says, "*Reveal not their adornment except such as is outward.*" I have explained this. "*To cast their veils over their bosoms.*" We have also explained this. Again, "*Reveal not their adornment except to their husbands...*" There is nothing which is obligatory to cover before a woman's husband. "*...their fathers, their sons, the sons of their husbands, their brothers, their brothers' children and their sisters' children.*" It is clear up to here. There is no debate about the relations mentioned. But, then, four more relations are mentioned and there is a discussion as to what is meant. "Or their women or what their right hand owns or such men who attend to them not having sexual desire or children who have not yet attained knowledge of women's private parts."

Does "or their women" mean all women? Or only Muslim women? Or women who live in their home and serve them? The third is highly unlikely and the possibility should not even be allowed that it be this because it makes no sense that among all women it only refers to women who work in their house. It would mean they would need to cover before women who are not their servants and clearly this is not so. One of the things which is certain from the beginning of Islam is that a woman is *mahram* to another woman. Thus one of the first two possibilities remain. First, "their women," refers to all women. Thus there is no woman who is not *mahram* for another woman. But, if it is the second one, that is, Muslim women, then non-Muslim women are not *mahram*.

Of course this is something for which perhaps some have issued a religious edict about but it is not this way. Some say it is forbidden for a Muslim woman to become naked before a non-Muslim woman. The reason is that it is not permitted for any woman to describe the body of another woman for her husband. This duty itself is sufficient for Muslim women but other women do not follow this. It is either obligatory or approved for a Muslim woman not to become naked before a non-Muslim woman who may go to her own husband and describe the Muslim woman's physical qualities.

At any rate, this is disapproved. It is difficult to say if it is forbidden because the verse itself does not say directly: Muslim women. Or who "what their right hands own" is. Here there are two possibilities. One is that female slaves are referred to. That is, it is not necessary for women to cover themselves from their female slaves or that it is not necessary for women to cover themselves from their slaves even if it be a male. This would mean that a male slave is *mahram*. Of course, this should not seem strange. If this were to be considered strange, stranger than this is that it is absolutely not obligatory for female slaves. That is, a female slave does not need to cover here head before anyone, her master or anyone else.

Here the verse refers to a woman and her own male slaves. If a woman has a male slave, is it obligatory for her to relate to him as a *mahram* or a non-*mahram*? This is one of those places where the traditions and the external form of the verse dictates that it is not obligatory to cover but the religious edicts lack harmony in this area. We say 'external form' of the verse because it is very difficult to consider female slaves in this verse. What about the female slaves of others? Her husband's female slaves? Others? What about women who are not female slaves? No. We could say other women are included in "their women." If we allow that it be related to free

LESSON SIX: THE ISLAMIC HIJAB – PART IV

women, the meaning would be that among female slaves, only her own female slaves are *mahram*.

See where this would lead. Female slaves are *mahram* for men but a free woman has to cover herself from these very slave women. It is clear that this is not so. The verse means both male and female slaves. The reason is clear. Since the male slaves work inside the house and covering before them would cause great difficulty, they are *mahram*. There are a great many traditions to this effect.

"Or suck men as attend to them, not having sexual desire," are men who have no designs on women, men who are impotent. It is like mentally retarded individuals who do not distinguish these things. Another possibility has been given by commentators. Some have said those who have no physical needs for women include the eunuchs and they are *mahram*. There are many traditions to this effect. They were allowed within the *harems* and were considered as women because they had no sexual need for women.

Some have said that this also includes the poverty-stricken and the needy. What was the criterion? Those who said that the mentally retarded or ill were meant was because they do not distinguish between the sexes and they do not comprehend the attractive force which exists in women. They are like children. Those who said it also includes the eunuchs have said that the main emphasis is upon 1ack of sexual need'. That is, the criterion is not being retarded but rather not having the sexual need for women.

Those who said it includes the needy and poverty-stricken have said those who have no physical need for women. They are like the eunuchs or if not eunuch, they are under such circumstances that they have forgotten sexual desires. Of course, it is very unlikely that this latter group be accepted. It is clear that there are mentally ill who have no sense of discernment. The highest form would be those who become like an eunuch.

"Or children who have not yet attained knowledge of women's private parts." Does this mean the children of the ages of 7 or 8 or 10? Or does it mean children who still do not have power? That is, have not reached puberty? The second has been taken by the religious jurisprudents and edicts issued accordingly. Until the time of puberty, they are *mahram* and after that time they are not *mahram*.

THE CONCLUSION OF VERSE 24:31

"Nor let them stamp their feet so that their hidden ornament may be known." Arab women stamped their feet so that their silver or gold anklets would make sounds and things hidden would appear. They are told not to do this, not to do something to draw the attention of others towards them. Thus in women's relations with unrelated non-*mahram* men, they should not do anything to draw attention towards themselves whether it be in the way they walk, in the way they talk, in their perfume or cosmetics. We had mentioned collyrium, for instance. It was an exception but it should not be so severe that it stimulates men and attracts them towards her and all should return to God, a command from God. Remember God. Return to God. God is aware of intentions. If we consider exceptions they are all under the condition that one's intentions be pure.

LESSON SEVEN

THE ISLAMIC HIJAB - PART V

SEEK PERMISSION TO ENTER ON THREE OCCASIONS

"*O believers! Let those your right hands own and those of you who have not reached puberty ask permission (before they come to your presence) at three times: before the ritual prayer of dawn and when you put off your outer garments at noon; and after the late night prayer; three times of undressing for you. Outside these times it is not wrong for you or for them to move about attending to each other; thus does God make clear the Signs for you, for God is All-knowing, All-wise. But when your children reach puberty let them (also) ask for permission as do those senior to them (in age). Thus does God make clear His signs for you for God is All-knowing, All-wise. Such women as are past childbearing age and have no hope of marriage, there is no blame on them if they put aside their (outer)garments, provided they make not a wanton display of their beauty; but it is best for them to be modest and God is All-hearing, All-knowing.*" (24:58-60)

These three verses mention two or three exceptions. One of the exceptions is in the first verse which we had previously related, "If you enter houses, say, 'Peace'." No one has the right to enter the house of another without first announcing one's entrance and receiving permission; even a child has no right to enter the house of his mother or sister without permission. It is only the husband who does not need to announce his arrival. Home is a place which a

LESSON SEVEN: THE ISLAMIC HIJAB - PART V

woman considers to be her place of retreat and she is usually dressed in such a way that she does not want anyone but her husband to see her as such.

In the past, the doors of homes were kept open and they were not considered to be places of retreat. The places of retreat were particular only to the rooms. It can be said that the ruling which previously related to rooms now rules for a house. It is customary now to have the door or the home closed and a woman may even consider her courtyard to be part of her place of retreat unless others have a view into it.

We have previously mentioned this ruling. There is no exception to it, whether a son is going to his mother's house or a daughter is going to her father's house, they must receive permission to enter the part that is considered to be a retreat.

We had another issue in the next verse about people who are exceptions so that women do not need to cover before them. The amount of the modest dress that is required for people who are not *mahram*, "their fathers...or their women or what their right hands own or children...," and then we discussed whether it meant only male slaves or included female slaves as well.

We pointed out that the external form of the verse reveals those who are the exceptions. Traditions, in particular, Shi'ite traditions, have said that they are the male servants. But the other problem is that among the Islamic scholars, perhaps, there are very few people who have issued an edict saying that male slaves are *mahram* within the home. That is, the ruling is that it is not necessary for women to cover themselves before them because they are taken as *mahram* but the external meaning of the verse is clear and the traditions say the same.

In these verses there are other exceptions about what the right hand owns and children because we had the exception that in the place of retreat of women, everyone, except her husband, must seek permission to enter. Here two other groups are mentioned as exceptions to this rule other than at the special times mentioned in the Holy Qur'an; first is "what their right hands own" and second are "children before they reach puberty."

Now as to "what their right hands own," let no one think that because there are no longer any slaves, there is no need to discuss this. No. We do not want to mention a duty of a slave here, but Islamic precepts in regard to slaves should be understood and if a person wants to reason from the verse itself, he can expand this ruling to include other than slaves.

As we pointed out, the verse said no one has the right to enter the home of another without first announcing it except those who are your slaves and children who have not yet reached puberty. These people are exceptions to seeking permission to enter a woman's retreat unless it occurs at the three special times mentioned.

The three times mentioned are times when a woman is most often not wearing her normal clothes. One of the three times is before the dawn prayer when she has first woken up and has not yet fully dressed. They have no right to enter without announcing their entrance. Another time is the middle of the day when it is very hot, when you come home and take off your clothes. They must seek

LESSON SEVEN: THE ISLAMIC HIJAB - PART V

permission to enter. The third is at night after the night prayer which is the time for going to sleep.

To sum up, at times other than when a woman normally takes off her clothes, and is a time of rest, they can enter without permission. Then the verse itself analyzes this. If you recall, two weeks ago, we mentioned these exceptions other than the husband; perhaps a father can also be included who is *mahram*, a woman's father-in-law and perhaps one's husband's son for which exceptions exist for covering various areas such as the face and hands. It is not the criterion that, at other times, are stimulating areas and a man whose eyes fall on the body of a woman or on her face presents a danger. But if we extend these criteria further, we will create difficulties. We have mentioned this.

Here, there is one sentence which shows why these are exceptions because it is their work to "move about attending to each other." A child who has not yet reached puberty, who is within the house, is continuously moving about. If the child has to continuously seek permission, it is very difficult. Thus, only at the special times should these exceptions seek permission.

And, now another issue. In the verse, "what their right hands own," are they female or male slaves? We said male slaves. In this area, again, the traditions have said this. In *al-Kafi* it has been recorded from Imam Sadiq (as): "What is meant is male slaves who do not have to seek permission except at the three times." Not female slaves because women are *mahram* to women. They asked, "Do women need to seek permission at these three times?" He said, "No. It is not necessary."

There is another tradition in which it is questionable if female slaves are meant but male slaves are clearly indicated.

It can be said that men are meant and not women in this verse because here the pronoun is exclusive to the masculine. They are the slaves of these women and we could say, perhaps, only women are meant but here the masculine plural appears. That is, those men who are your slaves do not need to get permission other than at those three times. Thus they are clearly; *mahram* and does this abrogate the other? No. Whatever is said in the other verse that male slaves and children who have not reached puberty are *mahram* is the same here. These two, then, correspond and this also corresponds with what has appeared in the traditions, in particular, Shi'ite traditions. Of course, they do not con form with the religious edicts.

Let us move beyond this. Those who are "what their right hands own," must not seek permission and also sons who have not reached puberty except at three times. The masculine plural is referred to and not women. Their work is to move about attending to each other; thus does God make clear the signs for you..."

"When your children reach puberty," they must always seek permission to enter. "Thus does God make clear His signs for you." The two exceptions which we had, one was in relation to male slaves and the other in relation to children who have not attained puberty. The third exception is "such women as are past child-bearing age."

"SUCH WOMEN AS ARE MENOPAUSIC..."

In the previous section, it was said that women had to cover themselves and not reveal their adornment except that which is outward and what is meant is the face and hands. In the next sentence, they are told to cover their necks with their scarf except women who are past child-bearing age.

If we compare this verse to the previous one, it is clear that women have two layers of clothes, the outer and the inner. In the former verse, "When you take off your outer garments," is again referred to here. Thus a woman can take off her outer garment. Beyond this? No. They can take off their outer clothes but they must not draw attention to themselves.

Even though all of these exceptions exist, it is better if a woman does not show herself to a man. It is better if a man does not look at a woman. These exceptions are because of needs that may arise. Islam is not a religion which wants to cause fault or blame to its followers. When there is no necessity or need or difficulty, it is better to observe the modest dress.

As I mentioned before, perhaps there is a class that men and women want to attend. Both will benefit from it but they do not need to be in the same room. It is better if they are in separate rooms. Here, at the same time that women have reached a certain age is an exception, it it still better if they do not, for instance, take off their outer garment and they remain like other Muslim women. God is All-knowing.

A PARTICULAR REFERENCE TO THE WIVES OF THE HOLY PROPHET

We have two more verses in *Surah Ahzab* which we will refer to and then we will end our discussion on the modest dress.

ON THE ISLAMIC HIJAB

One verse relates to the particularities of the wives of the Holy Prophet. Before Islam, in the houses of the people, according to the custom, there was no modest dress. There was complete intermixing of men and women. The people were, then, not accustomed to announcing their entrance. They would enter the home of the Holy Prophet (swas) unannounced and go through all of the rooms and if they were invited to dinner, it would be hours before they left.

They would stretch out their legs and begin to hold long discussions. This bothered the Holy Prophet (swas) and he was embarrassed to ask them to leave. Then verse 33:53 was revealed:

"And when you ask (his wives) for something you want, ask them from behind a curtain (hijab). That makes for greater purity for your hearts and theirs." (33:53)

Whenever the *'ulama* referred to the verse on the modest dress they meant this verse. This is what the word *hijab* means. The word *hijab* here has nothing to do with the word *hijab* which we refer to when we say women should cover such and such parts of their body. Thus this has nothing to do with our discussion and refers to people who should not enter the house of the Holy Prophet (swas) without announcing their entrance and if they want something, they should take it from behind a curtain.

THE VERSE ON THE OUTER GARMENT (JILBAB)

But there is another verse in this *Surah* which relates to our discussion.

"O Prophet! Say to your wives and daughters and the believing women that they draw their outer garments (jilbab) close

LESSON SEVEN: THE ISLAMIC HIJAB - PART V

to them; so it is more proper that they may be known and not hurt. God is All forgiving, All-compassionate. Now, if the hypocrites do not give over and those in whose hearts there is a sickness and they make commotion in the city, We shall assuredly set you against them and then they will be your neighbors there only for a little while." (33:59-60)

All of the commentators agree that there were certain events occurring to which this verse is related to in Madinah. There was a group of hypocrites and corrupt people who bothered people and, in particular, slave women. Then when they were asked why they were doing this, they said, "We thought they were slave women."

Slave women are among the exceptions. They do not need to cover themselves from non-*mahram* men and if they had outer garments, they did not wear it in a way to cover their hair. Very often Muslim women would walk down the street at night and this group of hypocrites would bother them. When they were caught, they would always use the excuse that they thought the women were slave women.

The verse was revealed for them to cover themselves and in this way be recognized so the hypocrites would not bother them or, at least, they would no longer have that excuse.

Some have commented on this verse in a different way. They say that it means that the women be recognized that they are not this way (to be bought and sold) because they say if a woman maintains her honor and respect and has a serious attitude about herself, even hypocrites will show her respect. If they know that she is not among the other women and if she conducts herself with dignity, they will not bother her.

Thus this verse refers to particular events which had occurred (and they are told to make their clothes a sign so that they be recognized apart from slave women). Then the verse threatens those who bother others, that if they do not desist, "We will set you against them."

Now let us see what limits were set so that they are recognized as being separate from the slave women. The verse says, "Draw your outer garments close to them." How close? They said they must cover their heads and some even said their chins so that this be their sign of difference with slave women.

It is not very clear exactly what the *jilbab* looked like. In the *Munjid* it says it is a loose flowing dress. If it were a dress, this verse would not then be telling them to cover their hair. Raghib Isfahani in the *Mufridat*, which is a very reliable book on the definition of words, having defined the words of the Holy Qur'an very well, says that it means both dress and scarf.

There is a tradition from Imam Reza (as), about women who are beyond a certain age, from which it becomes clear that it was something which covered the head. He said they may put aside the *jilbab*; there is no problem if one looks at the hair of an old woman. Here it is not clear if the *jilbab* covered the hair and the head.

In another tradition it would appear that the *jilbab* differed from the *khamur* but the difference is not clear. Perhaps it was larger. Imam Sadiq (as) was asked what these women can take off and he said their *jilbab* and *khamur*, i.e., their outer garment and scarf.

LESSON SEVEN: THE ISLAMIC HIJAB - PART V

There are two points which can be made use of in this verse. The first is that this verse adds nothing more to the verse from *Surah Nur*. Why? Because the verse refers to particular events which were occurring at that time, not a total ruling for all times and secondly, the verse just says to draw the *jilbab* closer to themselves.

EPILOGUE

THE PARTICIPATION OF WOMEN IN MEETINGS AND GATHERINGS

From what has been referred to in these lessons, it can be seen that, in the first place, Islam is concerned with and is attentive to the importance, extraordinary value and necessity for the legitimacy of sexual relations between men and women, whether it be concerned in their touching each other, hearing each other or living together. It is such that Islamic precepts would never allow the slightest detriment in whatever form it may take to be applied to it. But the world today overlooks this extraordinary human value and consciously chooses to ignore this point of view.

The world today, in the name of freedom of women, and, more directly, the freedom of sexual relations, has only served to corrupt the morale of the youth. Instead of this freedom helping to develop the amazing potentialities which exist within every human being, it wastes human energies and talents, in a way which did not exist in the past. Women have left their homes, but for what? For the cinema, the beach, the streets, and evening entertainment! In the name of freedom, women today have destroyed their homes without having effectively cultivated schools or universities or places of work.

As a result of this unrestrainedness and ignoring of any restrictions, the educational efficiency of young people, in general, has decreased. Young people run away from school and education

EPILOGUE

and sexual crimes have increased at enormous rates. The cinema market is doing a brisk business and the pockets of capitalists who deal in cosmetics are overflowing.

The second point is that in spite of the dangers which result from the breaking of the barriers of sexual modesty, the Divinely bestowed religious precepts of purity have not been heeded by them, as they guide the ummah towards moderation, far from any extremity. To the point that women are not drawn towards corruption, the Islamic precepts do not prevent her active participation in society. In some cases, it is even obligatory that she should participate, like in the *Hajj* rituals that are equally obligatory upon men and women. No husband has the right to prevent it.

As we know, it is not obligatory for women to participate in the *jihad* unless a city or an area of Muslims has been attacked and the *jihad* has a totally defensive nature.[1] Then, just as the edicts of the religious jurisprudents state, the *jihad* becomes obligatory on women as well. Otherwise, it is not obligatory. Even so, the Holy Prophet (swas) gave some women permission to participate in the battles to help the soldiers and the wounded. There are many stories of this in the history of Islam.[2]

It is not obligatory upon women to participate in the congregational ritual prayers but if they go, it becomes obligatory upon them to participate and not to leave.[3]

---

[1] *Masalik*, the section on *jihad*.
[2] *Sahih Muslim*, vol. 5, pp.196-97; *Sunan Abu Dawud*, vol. 2, p. 17; *Jama'h Tirmizi*, p. 247.
[3] *Wasail al-Shiah*, vol.1, p. 456.

It is not obligatory for women to participate in the Festival ritual prayers but they are not forbidden from participating. It is disapproved for women of great respect or beauty to participate in such prayers.[4]

The Holy Prophet (swas) cast lots among his wives and would take them with him on his journeys and some of his companions also took their wives.[5]

The Holy Prophet (swas) would accept the allegiance of women but he did not shake hands with them. He would order a bowl of water to be brought. He would put his hand in the water and order the women offering her allegiance to do the same thing. She was considered as having pledge her allegiance.[6] Ayesha said that throughout his lifetime the Holy Prophet (swas) never touched the hands of a woman who was not *mahram*.

He did not forbid women from participating in burial ceremonies although he also did not feel it was necessary. He preferred that they do not participate although, under special circumstances, they did so and possibly participated in the recitation of the ritual prayers. It has been narrated in our traditions that when Zaynab, the oldest daughter of the Holy Prophet (swas) died,

---

[4] *Wasail al-Shiah*, vol.1, p. 474.

[5] *Sahih Muslim*, vol. 7, p. 437.

[6] All historians and commentators have recorded this. Histo-rians recorded it in recalling the events of the victory of Makkah and commentators have referred to it when commenting upon the verse, "*O Prophet! When believing women come to you to take the oath of allegiance...*" (60:12). See also *Al-Kafi*, vol. 5, p. 526.

EPILOGUE

Fatimah, peace be upon her, and other Muslim women came and recited the ritual prayer for her.[7]

According to Shi'ite traditions, it is disapproved for young girls to participate in mourning ceremonies. Sunni scholars have recorded from Umm Atiyyah who said that the Holy Prophet (swas) encouraged women not to participate in mourning processions but he did not forbid it.[8]

Asma, the daughter of Yazid Ansari, was selected by the women of Madinah as their representative to go to the Holy Prophet (swas) to tell him of the complaints of the women of Madinah and receive his answer. When Asma entered, the Holy Prophet (swas) was seated among a group of the Companions.

She said, "May my mother and father be sacrificed for you. I am the representative of the women of Madinah to you. We women say that God almighty sent you as a Prophet to both men and women. You are not just the Prophet of the men. We women also found faith in you and God Almighty. We women sit in our homes meeting the sexual needs of men. We nourish your children in our wombs but we see that all of the sacred duties, great and valuable deeds which are regarded by God, are given to men alone and we are deprived. Men are allowed to gather together. They visit the sick. They participate in funeral processions. They repeatedly perform the *Hajj* rituals and above everything else, they are allowed to participate in the *jihad* in God's Way. Whereas when a man goes on the *hajj* or the *jihad*, it is we women who stay behind and protect

---

[7] *Wasail al-Shiah*, vol.1, p. 72.
[8] *Sahih Muslim*, vol. 3, p. 47; *Sahih Bukhari*, vol. 2, p. 94; *Sunan Abu Dawud*, vol. 2, p.180.

his poverty. We weave cloth for his clothes. We train his children. How is it that we are partners of you men in difficult tasks but when it comes to sacred duties and deeds for which God gives spiritual reward, we are not partners and we are deprived of all of them?

"The Holy Prophet (swas) looked at the Companions and asked, 'Have you ever heard a woman speak so well, so logically and so clearly about religious affairs?'

'The Holy Prophet (swas), turned to Asma and said, Woman! Try to understand what you are saying and explain to the women who sent you. Do you think that every man receives spiritual rewards and virtues for doing these things and women are deprived of them? No. This is not so. If a woman takes good care of her family and husband and does not allow the pure environment of her home to become polluted by the dust of darkness, she will receive spiritual rewards, virtues and successes equivalent to all of the work that men do.' "

Asma was a woman of faith. Her requests and those of the women who thought like her came from the depths of their faith, not out of lust or greed which we most often see today. She and the women who sent her were concerned that perhaps the duties which they performed had no value and that all of the sacred duties were particular to men. She and the women she represented wanted equality, but in what? In implementing the Divine commands and carrying out their religious duties. That which never entered their minds was a confrontation to gain individual egotistical desires in the name of a 'right'. Thus when she heard the response of the Holy

EPILOGUE

Prophet (swas), her face lighted up with pleasure and she returned in great happiness to her friends.⁹

As to the participation of women in these things, the traditions contradict one another. Some completely forbid it, but the author of *Wasa'il*, who was himself a reliable transmitter, noting the total collection of Islamic traditions, said, "It can be concluded from the totality of Islamic traditions that it is permissible for women to leave their homes to participate in mourning ceremonies or to see to the rights of the people¹⁰ or to attend a funeral procession and to participate in these gatherings just as Fatimah, peace be upon her, and the wives of the pure Imams, peace be upon them, participated in these kinds of ceremonies. Thus, the totality of the traditions rule that we ignore that which forbids it."¹¹

The Holy Prophet (swas) allowed his wives to leave their homes to meet the needs they had and do what they had to do.

It is recorded that the Holy Prophet (swas) ordered the door to the mosque for women be separate from the men's door so that men and women would not be obliged to go and come through the same door. He forbid men from using that door.¹²

It is also recorded that the Holy Prophet (swas) commanded that after the night prayer, women be allowed to leave the mosque

---

⁹ *Asad al-Ghabah*, vol. 5, pp. 338-399.
¹⁰ See *Bihar al-Anwar*, vol. 11, p. 118 where a tradition is recorded from *Al-Kafi* from Imam Musa ibn Ja'far (as), who said: "My father, Imam Ja'far (as), would send my mother and his mother to attend to the needs of the poor in Madinah."
¹¹ *Wasail al-Shiah*, vol.1, p. 72.
¹² *Sunan Abu Dawud*, vol.1, p. 109.

first so that they would not have to mix together.[13] In order that no contacts prevail, he said that women should walk down the side of the street and men, down the middle.[14]

It is because of this that religious jurisprudents issue edicts that it is disapproved for men and women to mix together. Ayatullah Sayyid Muhammad Kazim Tabatabai Yazdi wrote, "In truth, if a person was to look at Islam with an open mind, he or she would confirm that the way of Islam is the way of moderation. At the same time that Islamic precepts have provided the greatest extent of precautions to protect the purity and sanctity of sexual relations, in no way do they prevent the human talents of women from blossoming. As a matter of fact, these precepts provide for both the spirit to remain healthy and for family relations to be more intimate and serious as well as better preparing men and women for a healthy social environment, far from any extremes."[15]

---

[13] *Al-Kafi*, vol. 5, p. 519.
[14] *Sunan Abu Dawud*, vol.2, p. 658.
[15] *Urwat al-Wusqa*, chapter i, issue 49.

GLOSSARY

Ali Abu Talib, Imam (600-661 AD): The cousin and son-in-law of the Prophet, he was the fourth rightly-guided caliph and first pure Imam. The imamate (leadership) originates with him and he and eleven of his descendants are representatives of both the exoteric and esoteric dimension of Islam. According to the Shi'ites, he was selected at a place outside of Makkah called Ghadir Khumm by the Prophet as his 'entrusted' (*wasi*) and successor just after the Farewell Pilgrimage of the Prophet. The detail of Ghadir Khumm event is available at: https://www.al-islam.org/ghadir/

Age of Ignorance (*Jahiliyah*): The period of multitheism or polytheism, *kufr* and idolatry before the appearance of Islam (pre-Islamic era) and the revival of monotheism.

Ali Reza, Imam (765-818 AD): The eighth pure Imam who was chosen as the successor to the caliphate by the Abbasid al-Ma'mun but due to his immense popularity among the people, he was martyred by the caliph. He is buried in Mashhad which is a center of pilgrimage in Iran.

aurah: Refers to anything which is open, naked, unprotected and can be easily harmed and for which one is concerned as it is vulnerable. The body of a woman is referred to as *aurah* as it is vulnerable because it can be easily harmed and must be covered by some kind of protective covering such as clothes.

GLOSSARY

***dhimmah*:** People of the Book who live in Muslim lands and are accorded hospitality and protection by Islam on condition of acknowledging Islamic political domination and paying the *jizyah* tax.

Hasan Askari, Imam (846-874 AD): He was the eleventh pure Imam who lived in extreme secrecy in Samarra because of the continuous surveillance of the caliph's security forces. He married the daughter of the Byzantine Emperor, Nargis Khatun, who had embraced Islam and sold herself into slavery in order to enter the household of the Imam. From this marriage the twelfth Imam was born.

Hasan ibn Ali, Imam (625-670 AD): The second divinely appointed Imam from Ahlul Bayt (as) who was leader of *ummah* for a short period of time after the martyrdom of Imam Ali (as) before it was usurped by Mu'awiyah, the founder of the Umayyid dynasty.

Ja'far Sadiq, Imam (702-765 AD): The sixth pure Imam who continued the propagation of Shi'ite sciences to the extent that Shi'ite law is named after him. He taught over 4000 students including Abu Hanifah, the founder of one of the four Sunni schools of law.

***Mahram* and Non-*mahram*:** A man and a woman are related in two ways according to the Divine Law, either through close kinship, which is clearly stipulated in the Qur'an, or they are married to each other. That is, a man and a woman are related in the Divine Law if their kinship is too close for marriage or they are actually married. This is referred to as *mahram*. Non-*mahram* refers to a man and a woman who can marry each other.

Malik Ashtar: The governor of Egypt during the caliphate of Ali, peace be upon him, who wrote him a famous letter about how to rule people in a fair and just way.

Minbar: The place within a mosque from which a sermon is delivered, it is most often made of wood and consists of stairs leading to a flat seat upon which the speaker sits.

Muhammad Baqir, Imam (676-733 AD): The fifth pure Imam who was a well-known teacher of the religious sciences.

mujtahid: A person who engages in strenuous endeavor to reason a religious issue (*ijtihad*).

Musa ibn Ja'far, Imam (746-799 AD): The seventh pure Imam who faced extreme hardship due to the renewed opposition of the Abbasid caliphate against the Shi'ites.

Sunnah: The customs, behavior and traditions of the Prophet of Islam.

www.ingramcontent.com/pod-product-compliance
Lightning Source LLC
LaVergne TN
LVHW041609070526
838199LV00052B/3050